WOMEN OF POP &ROCK

7777 W. BLUEMOUND RD. P.O. BOX 13819 MILWAUKEE, WI 53213

Visit Hal Leonard Online at
www.halleonard.com

BAD ROMANCE

Words and Music by STEFANI GERMANOTTA
and NADIR KHAYAT

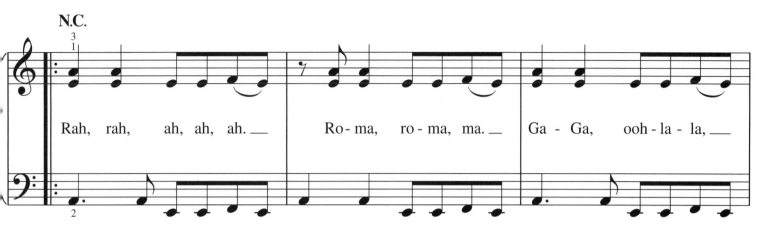

Rah, rah, ah, ah, ah. __ Ro-ma, ro-ma, ma. __ Ga-Ga, ooh-la-la, __

want your bad ro - mance.

{ I want your ug - ly, I want your dis - ease. __
{ I want your hor-ror, I want your de - sign __

I want your ev -'ry-thing as long as it's free. __ I want your love.)
'cause you're a crim-i - nal as long as you're mine. __ I want your love.)

Love, love, love, I want your love.

I want your love and I | want your re - venge, __ you and | me could write a bad ro -

mance. Oh, _____ | _____ I want your love and all your | lov-in's re - venge, __ you and

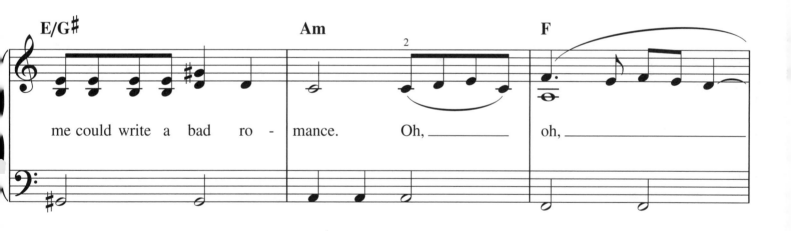

me could write a bad ro - | mance. Oh, _____ | oh, _____

_____ | caught in a bad ro - | mance. Oh, _____

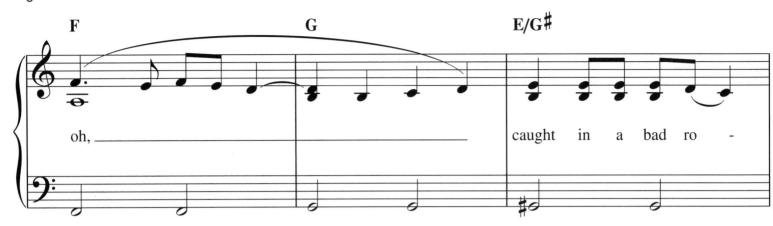

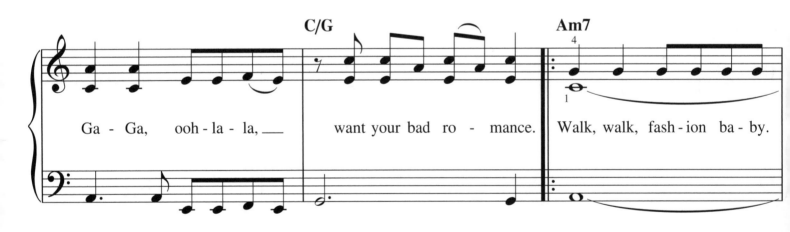

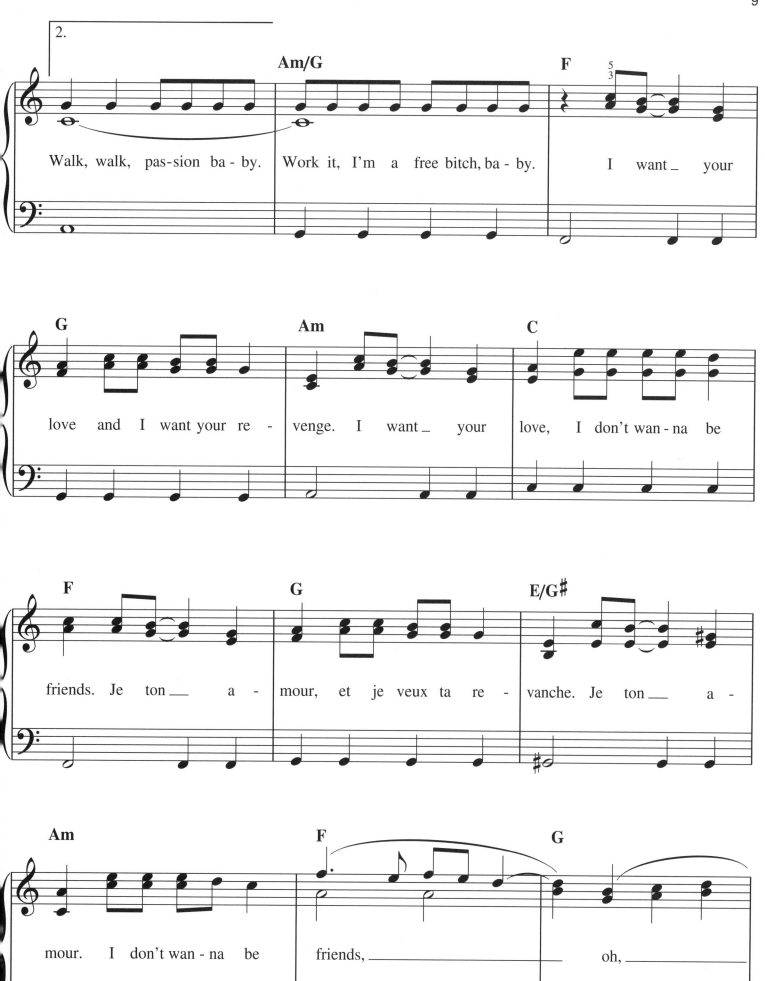

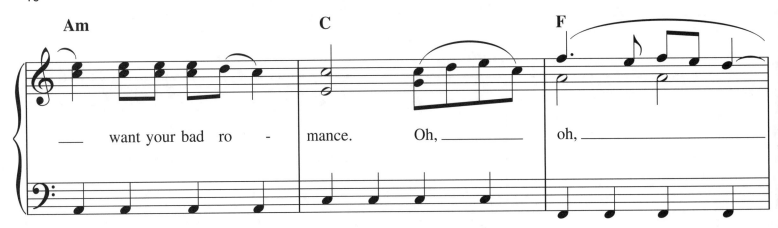

GIRL ON FIRE

Words and Music by ALICIA KEYS,
SALAAM REMI, JEFF BHASKER,
NICKI MINAJ and BILLY SQUIER

Oh, _____ she's got both feet on the ground __ and she's burn-ing it down. _

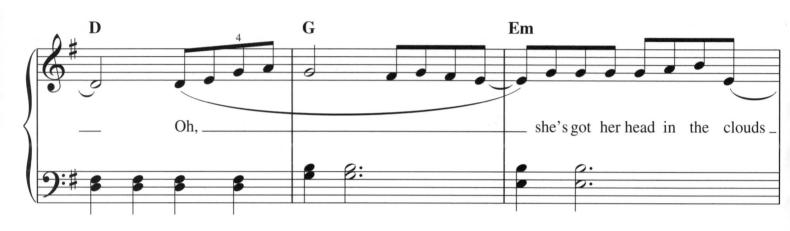

_ Oh, _____ she's got her head in the clouds _

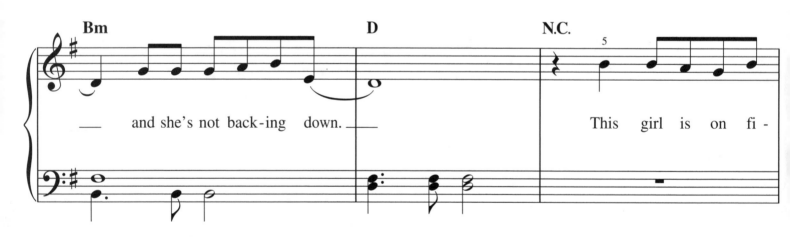

_ and she's not back-ing down. __ This girl is on fi -

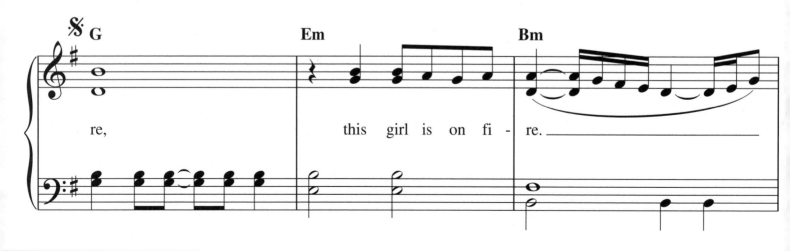

re, this girl is on fi - re. _____

She's walk-ing on fi - re.

This girl is on fi -

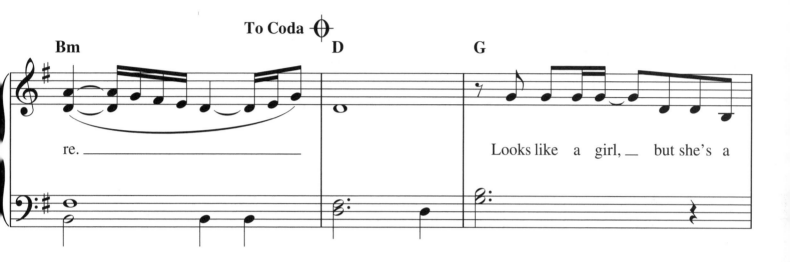

To Coda

re. _____

Looks like a girl, __ but she's a

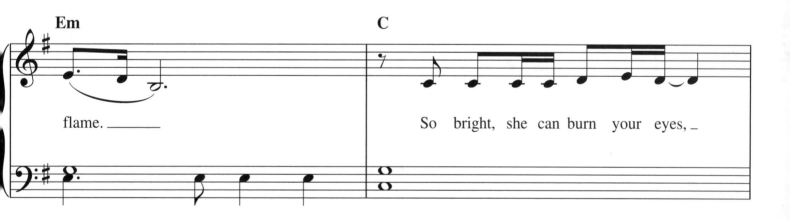

flame. _____

So bright, she can burn your eyes, __

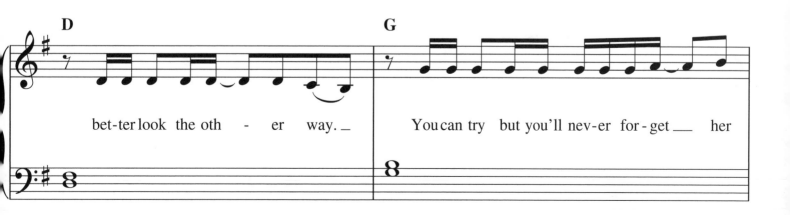

bet-ter look the oth - er way. __

You can try but you'll nev-er for-get __ her

name. _____   She's on top of the world, _   hot‑test of the hot‑test girls. _ Say

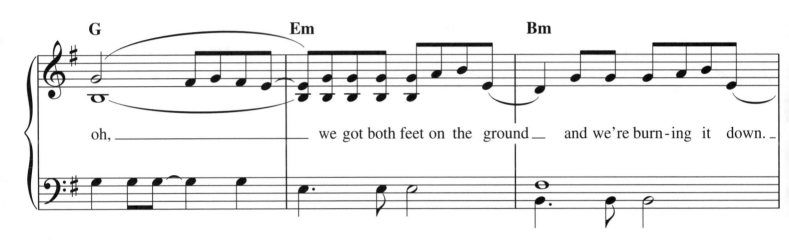

oh, _____   we got both feet on the ground _   and we're burn‑ing it down. _

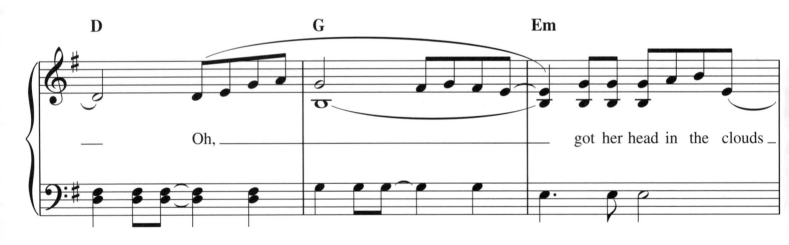

Oh, _____   got her head in the clouds _

D.S. al Coda

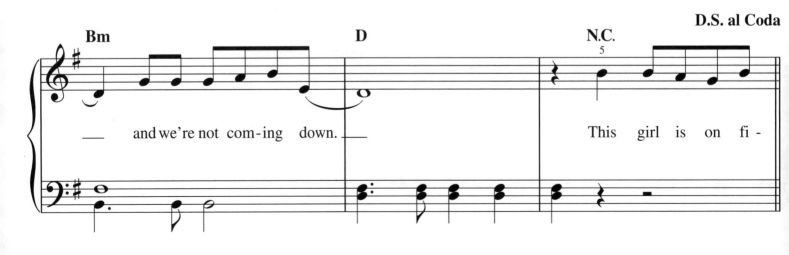

_ and we're not com‑ing down. _   This girl is on fi‑

15

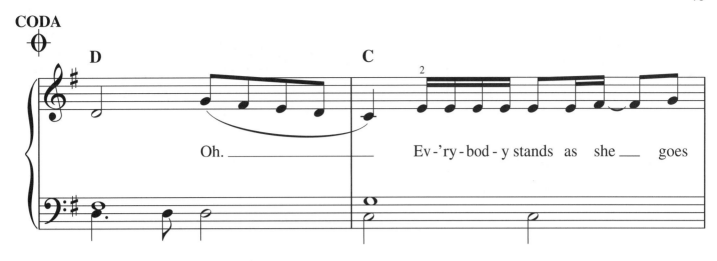

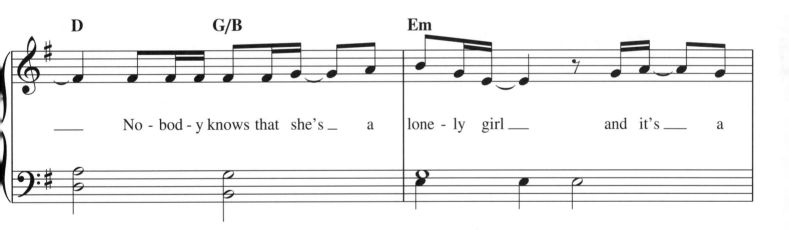

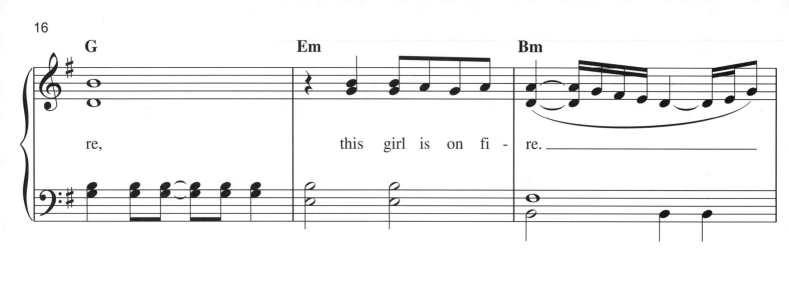

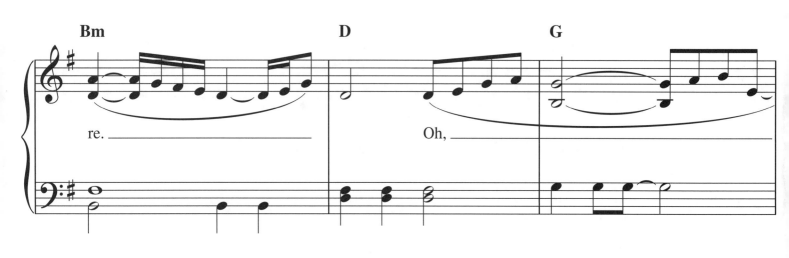

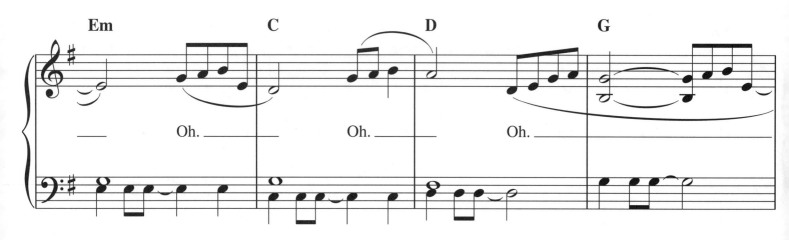

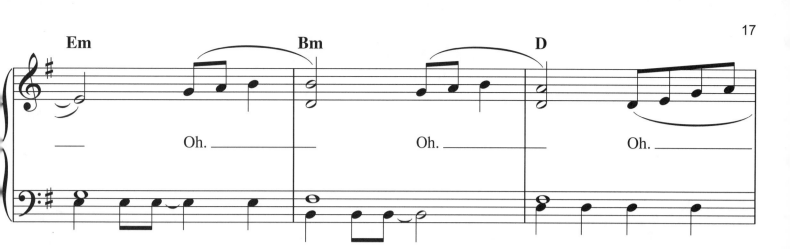

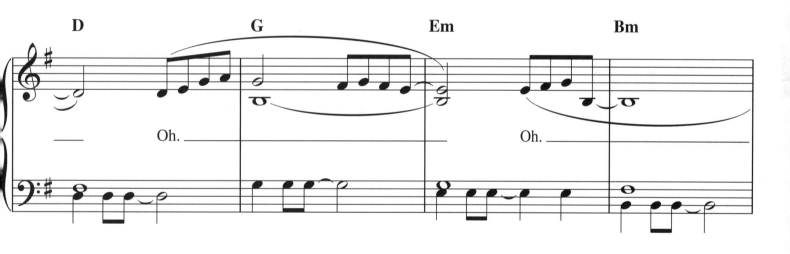

BLOW ME
(One Last Kiss)

Words and Music by ALECIA MOORE
and GREG KURSTIN

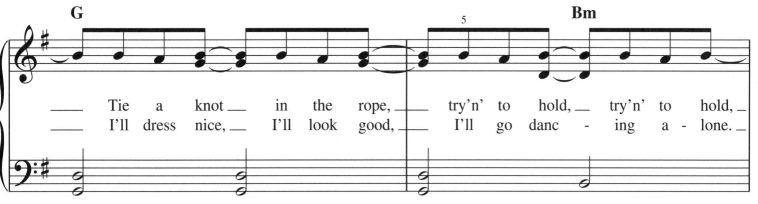

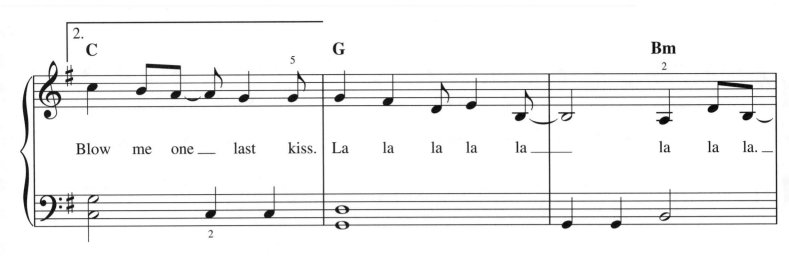

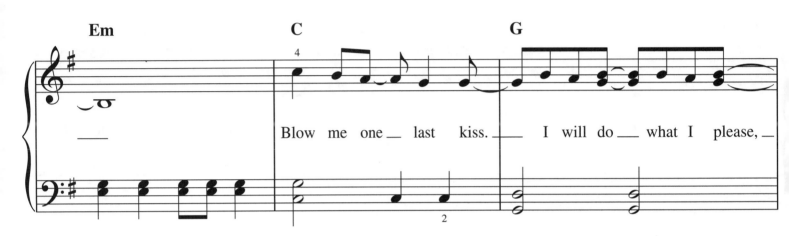

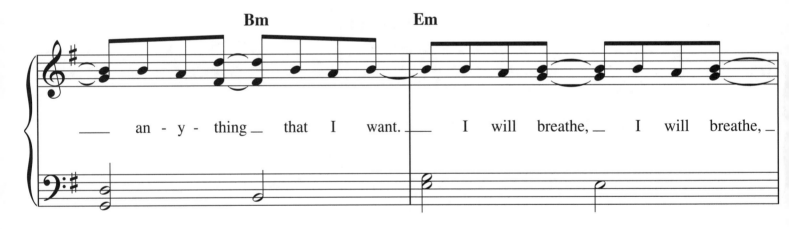

HALO

Words and Music by BEYONCÉ KNOWLES,
RYAN TEDDER and EVAN BOGART

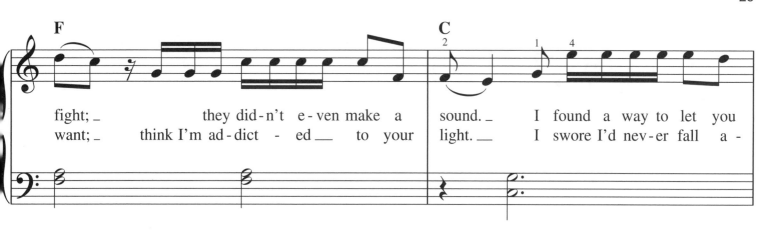

fight; _ they did-n't e - ven make a sound. _ I found a way to let you
want; _ think I'm ad - dict - ed _ to your light. _ I swore I'd nev-er fall a -

in, _ but I real - ly nev-er had a doubt. _ Stand - in' in the light of your ha -
gain, _ but this don't e - ven feel like fall - in'. Grav - i - ty _ can't _ for -

lo, ooh, _ I've got my an - gel now. _ It's like I've been a - wak - ened;
get _ to pull me back to the ground a - gain. Feels like I've been a - wak - ened; _

_ ev - 'ry rule I had you break - in'. _ It's the risk that I'm tak - in', _
_ ev - 'ry rule I had you break - in'. _ The risk that I'm tak - in', _

I ain't nev-er gon-na shut you out. ___
I'm nev-er gon-na shut you out. ___
Ev-'ry-where I'm look-in'

now, I'm sur-round-ed by your em-brace. ___ Ba-by, I can see your

ha-lo. _____ You know you're my sav-ing. grace. You're ev-'ry-thing I need and

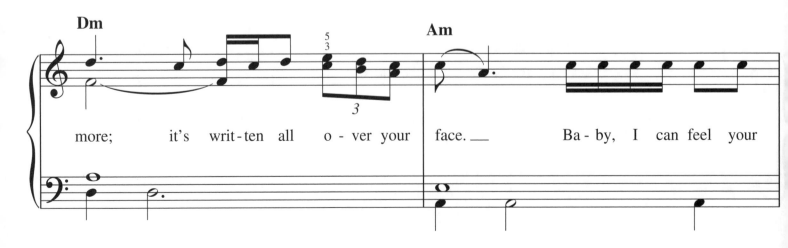

more; it's writ-ten all o-ver your face. ___ Ba-by, I can feel your

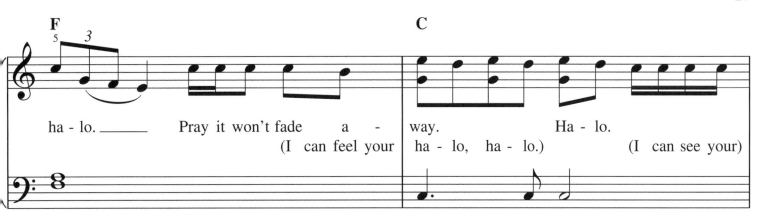

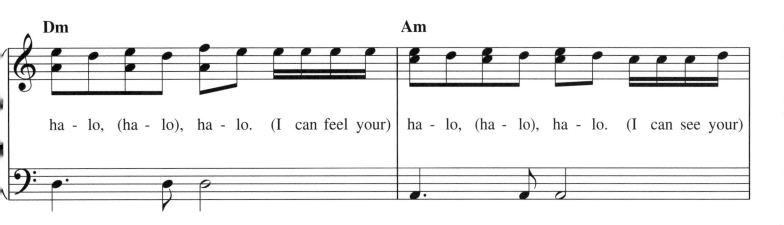

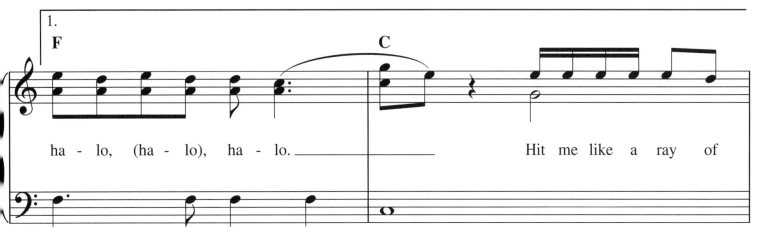

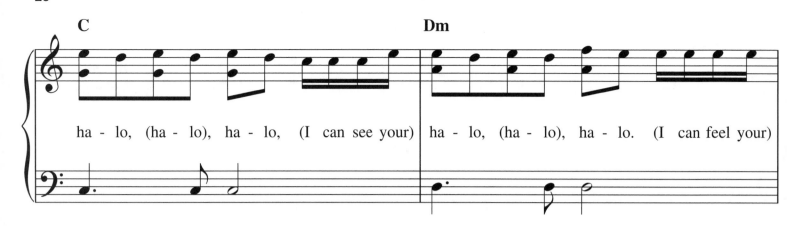

ha - lo, (ha - lo), ha - lo, (I can see your) ha - lo, (ha - lo), ha - lo. (I can feel your)

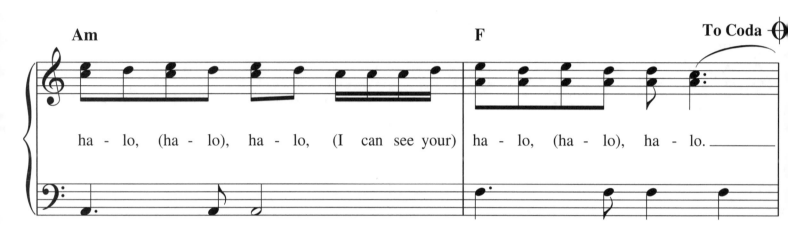

ha - lo, (ha - lo), ha - lo, (I can see your) ha - lo, (ha - lo), ha - lo.____

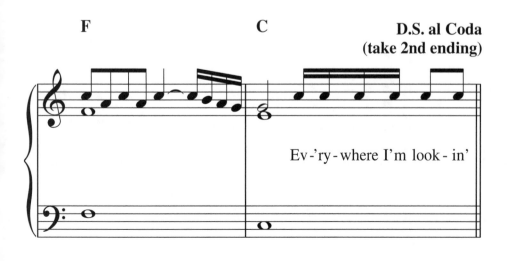

Ev-'ry-where I'm look-in'

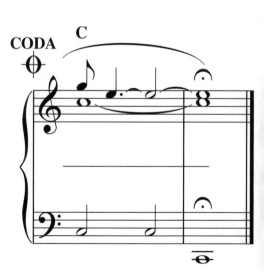

IF I AIN'T GOT YOU

Words and Music by
ALICIA KEYS

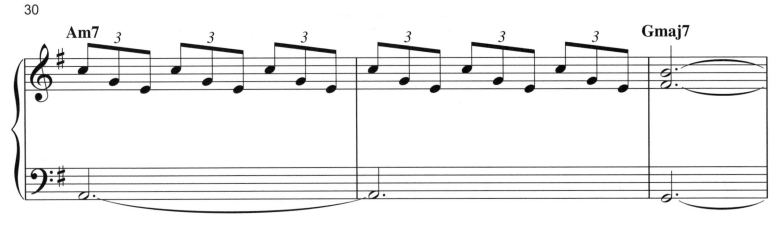

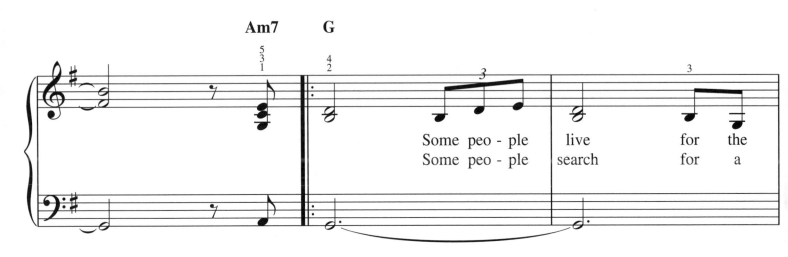

Some peo - ple live for the
Some peo - ple search for a

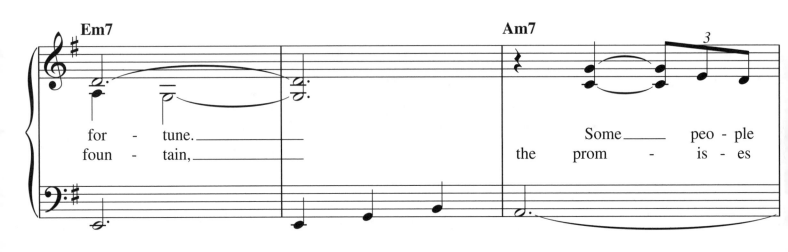

for - tune. Some____ peo - ple
foun - tain, the prom - is - es

live just for the fame. You know,____
for - ev - er____ young.

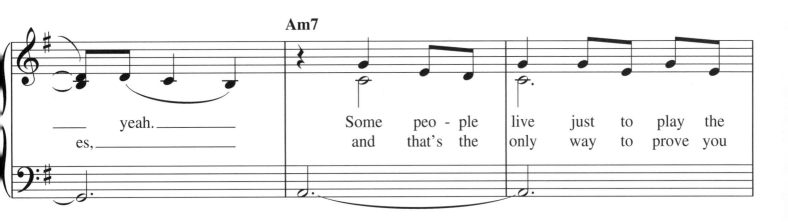

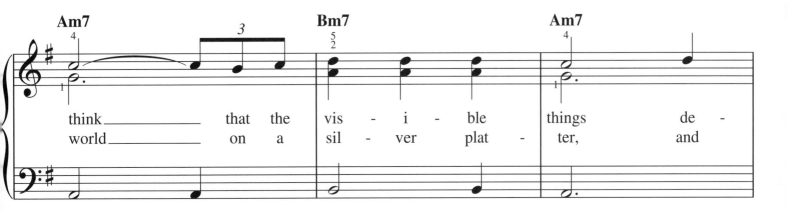

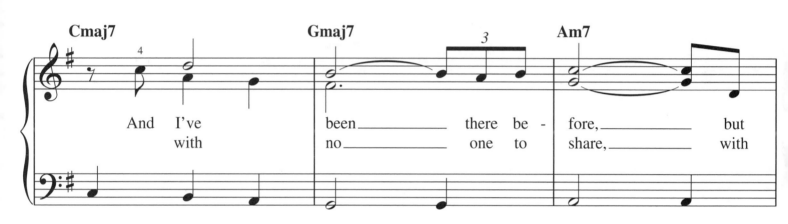

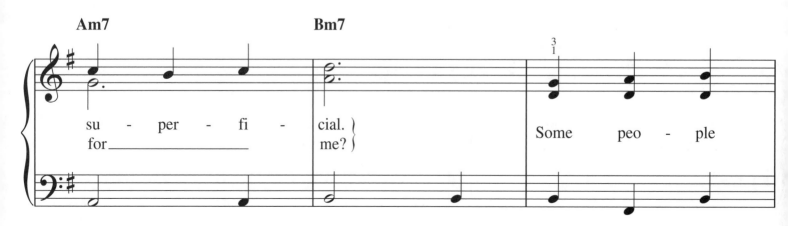

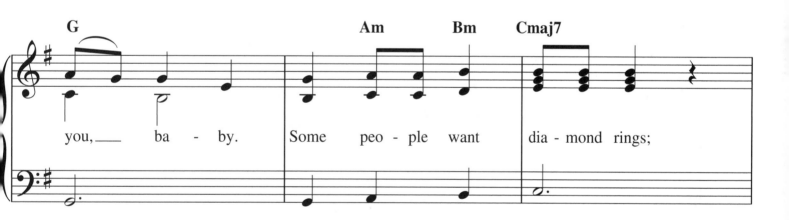

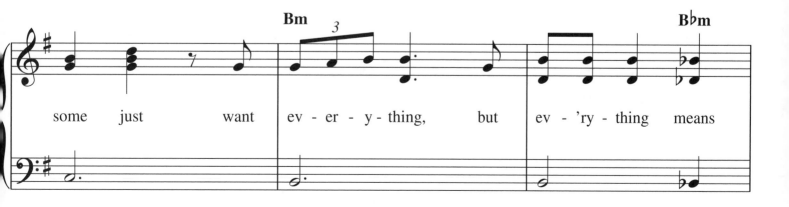

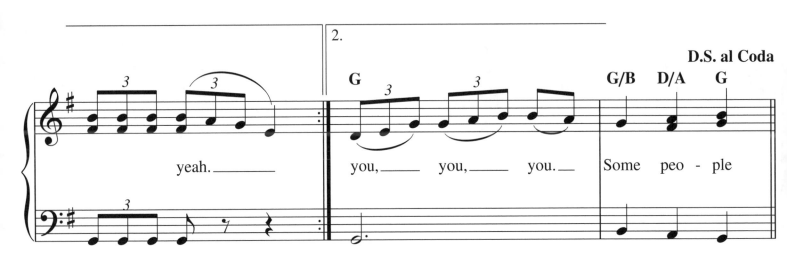

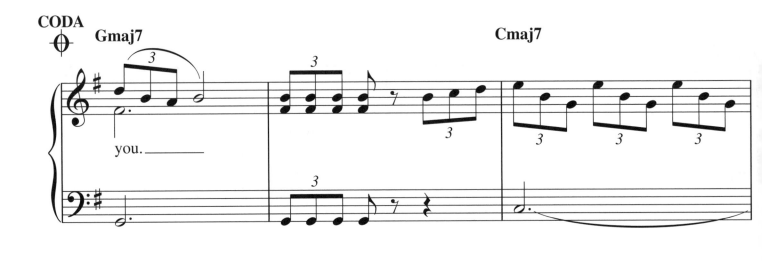

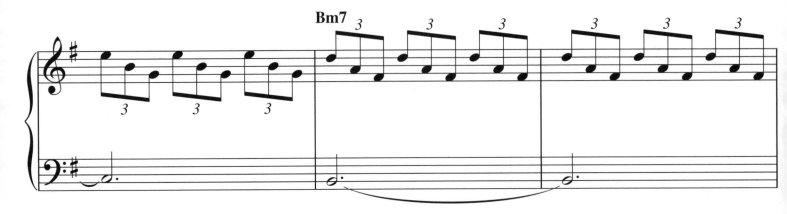

I KNEW YOU WERE TROUBLE.

Words and Music by TAYLOR SWIFT,
SHELLBACK and MAX MARTIN

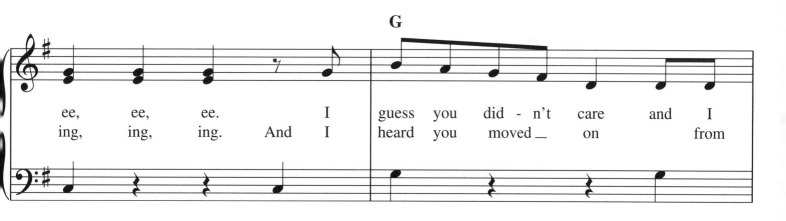

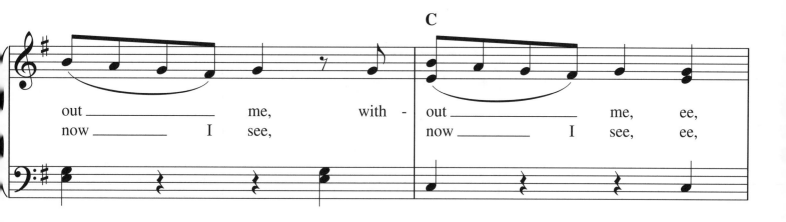

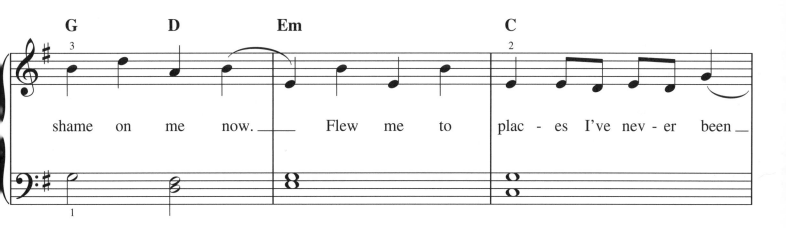

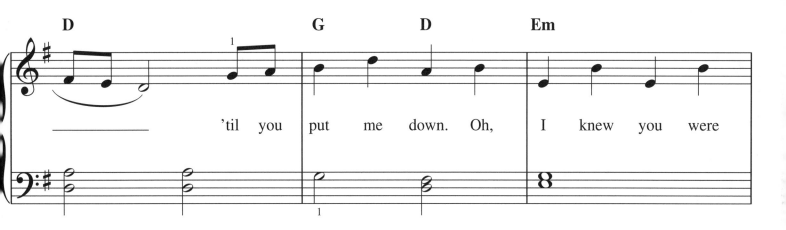

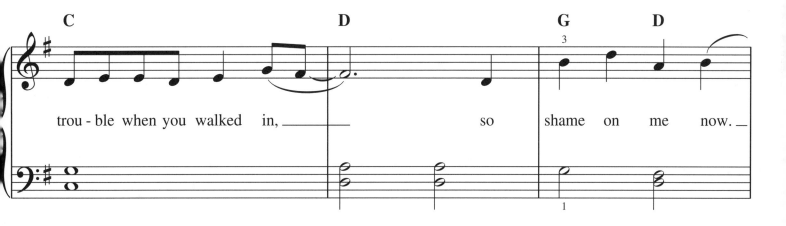

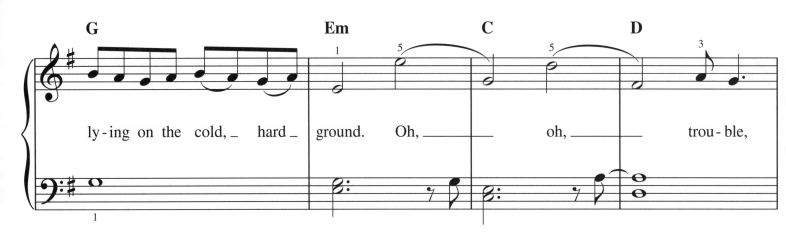

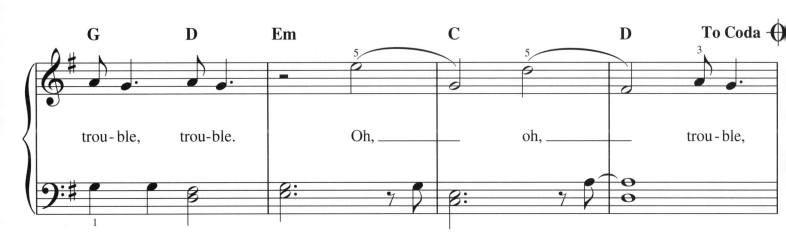

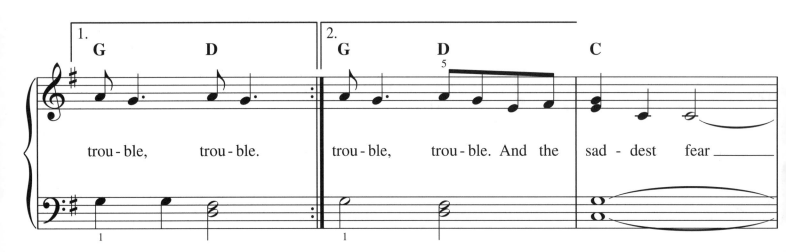

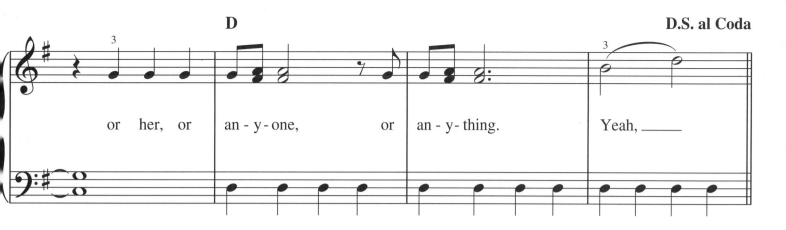

D.S. al Coda

or her, or an-y-one, or an-y-thing. Yeah, _____

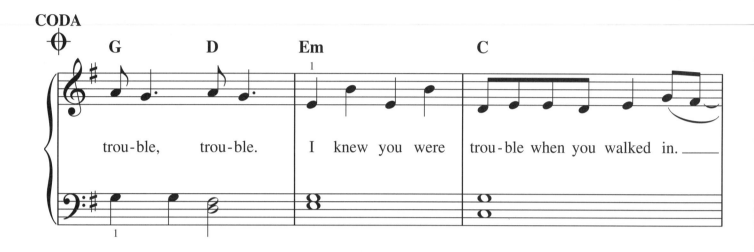

trou-ble, trou-ble. I knew you were trou-ble when you walked in. _____

_____ Trou-ble, trou-ble, trou-ble. I knew you were

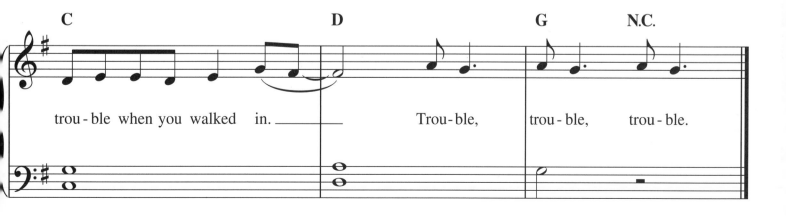

trou-ble when you walked in. _____ Trou-ble, trou-ble, trou-ble.

JAR OF HEARTS

Words and Music by BARRETT YERETSIAN,
CHRISTINA PERRI and DREW LAWRENCE

Moderate Ballad

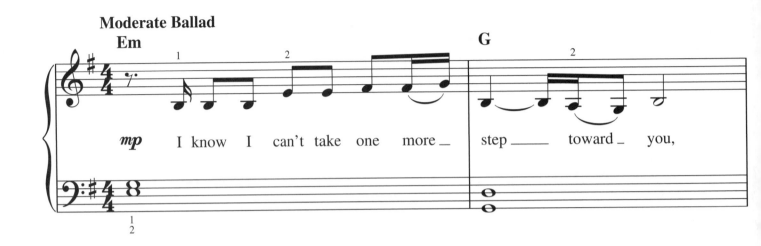

I know I can't take one more __ step __ toward __ you,

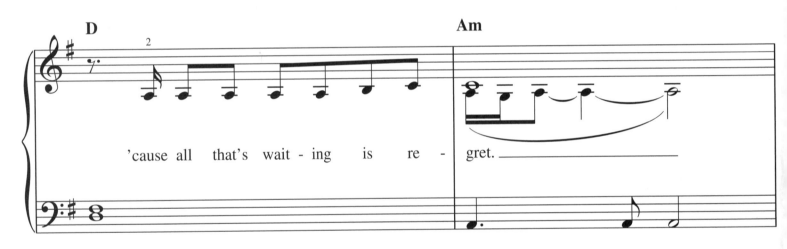

'cause all that's wait - ing is re - gret. __

And don't you know I'm not your __ ghost __ an - y - more,

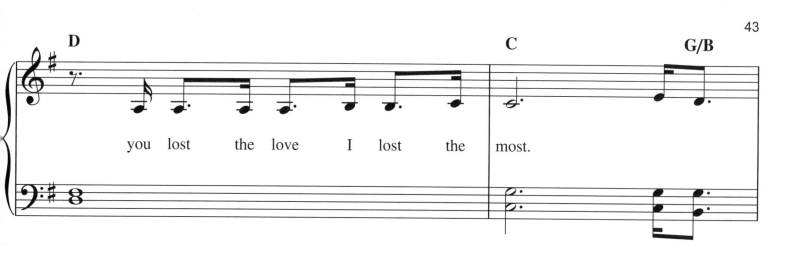

you lost the love I lost the most.

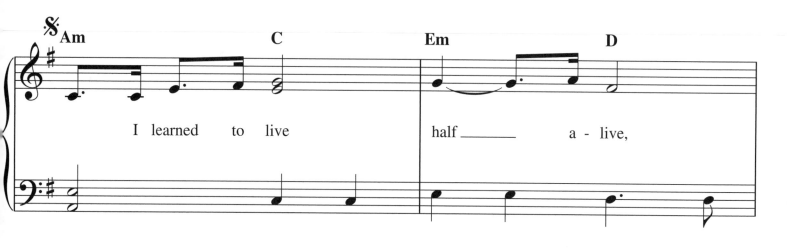

I learned to live half _____ a - live,

and now you want me one more _____ time. _____

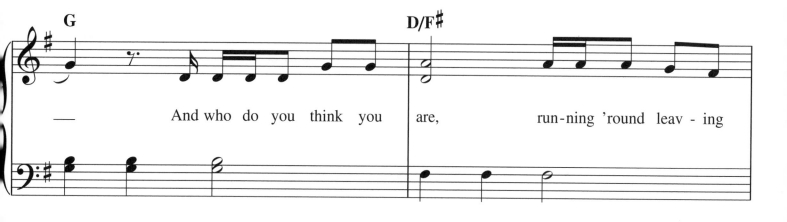

_____ And who do you think you are, run-ning 'round leav - ing

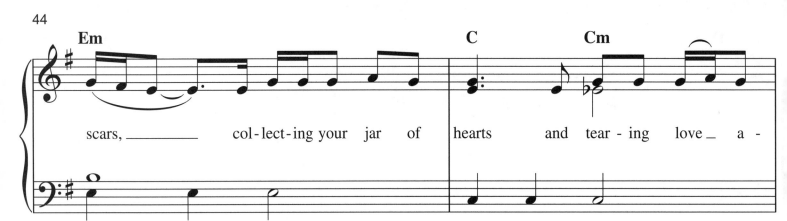

scars, _____ col-lect-ing your jar of hearts and tear-ing love _ a-

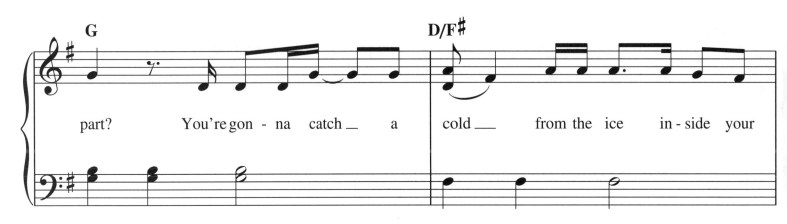

part? You're gon - na catch _ a cold _ from the ice in - side your

soul. _____ So don't come back for me. Who do you think you

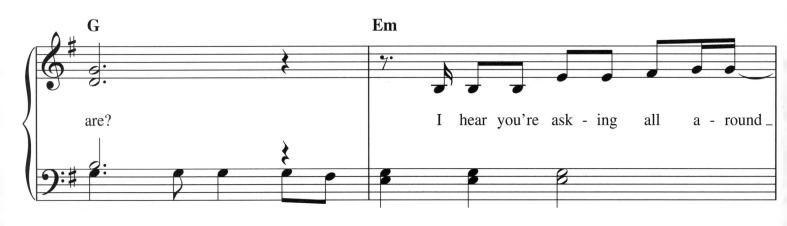

are? I hear you're ask - ing all a - round _

if I am an-y-where to ___ be

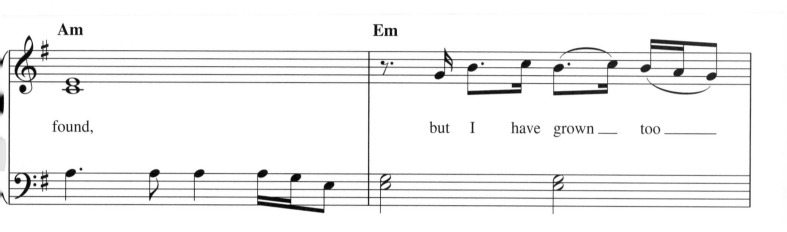

found, but I have grown ___ too ___

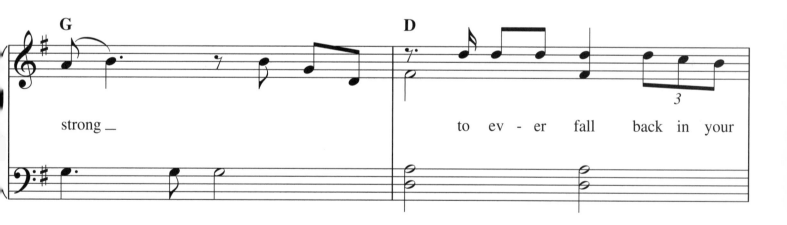

strong ___ to ev - er fall back in your

D.S. al Coda

CODA

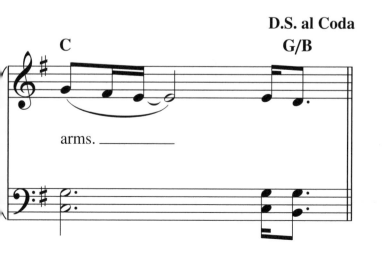

arms. ___

are? And

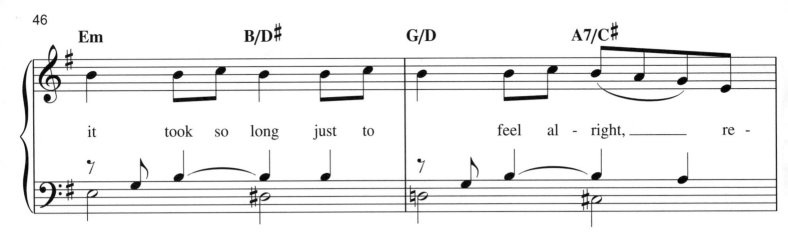

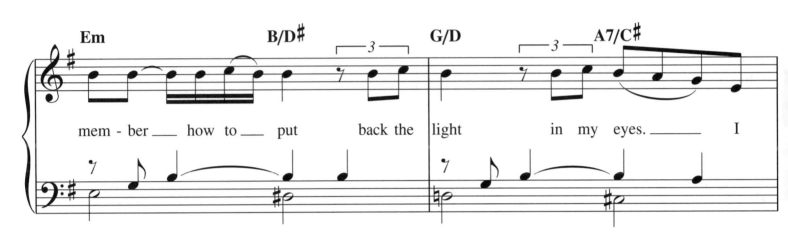

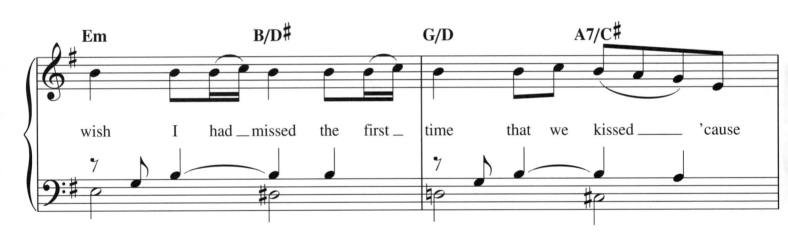

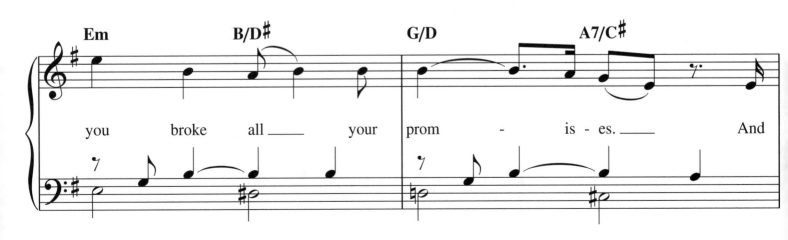

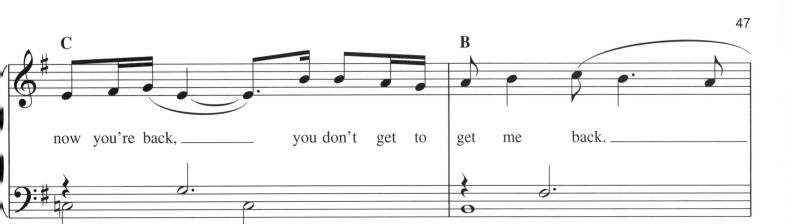

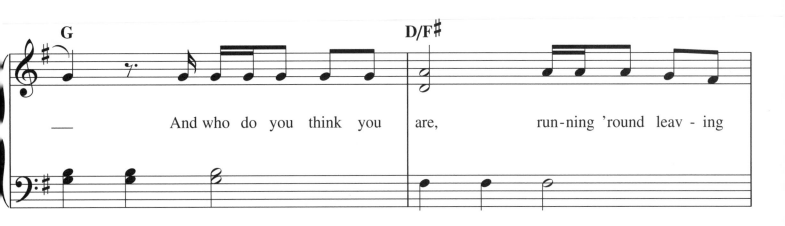

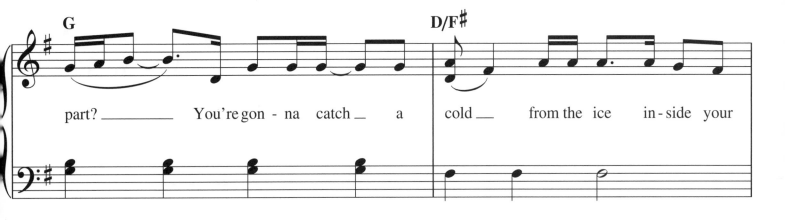

soul. _____ So don't come back for me, don't come back at

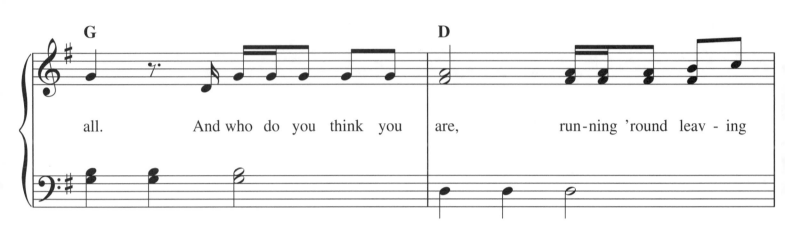

all. And who do you think you are, run-ning 'round leav-ing

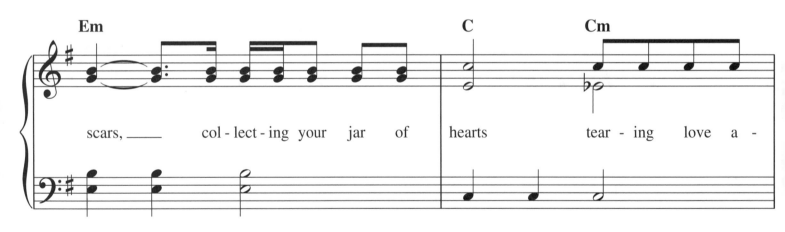

scars, _____ col-lect-ing your jar of hearts tear-ing love a-

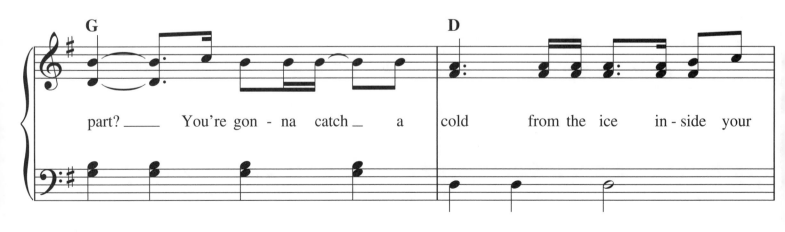

part? _____ You're gon-na catch _ a cold from the ice in-side your

soul. Don't come back __ for me, don't come back at

all. Who do you think you

are? _____ Who do you think you

are? _____ Who do you think you are?

rit.

KING OF ANYTHING

Words and Music by
SARA BAREILLES

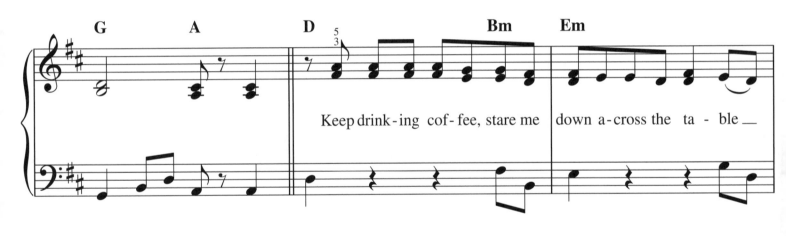

Keep drink-ing cof-fee, stare me down a-cross the ta - ble

while I look out - side. So man - y things I'd say if

on-ly I were a-ble, but I just keep qui-et and count the cars that pass by.

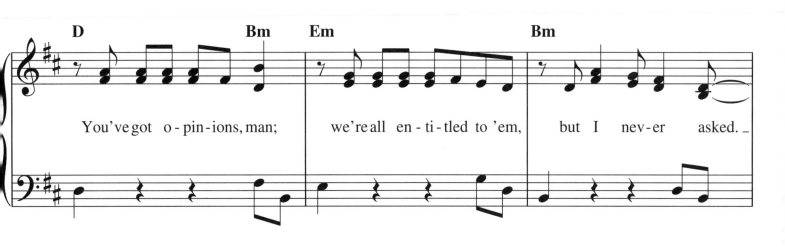

You've got o-pin-ions, man; we're all en-ti-tled to 'em, but I nev-er asked.

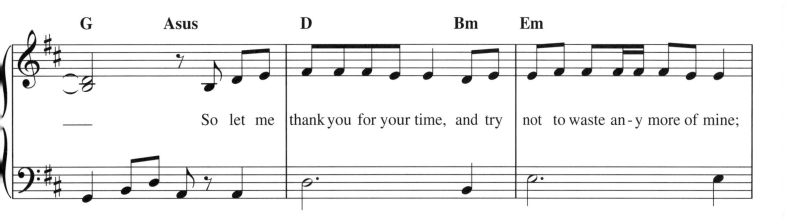

So let me thank you for your time, and try not to waste an-y more of mine;

get out of here fast. I hate to break it to you, babe,

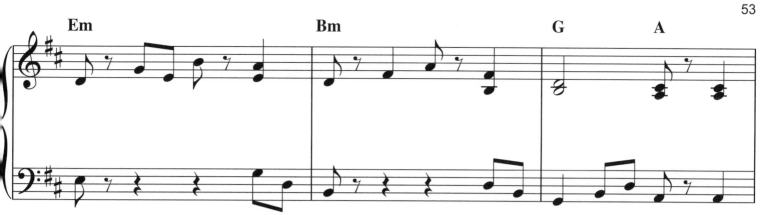

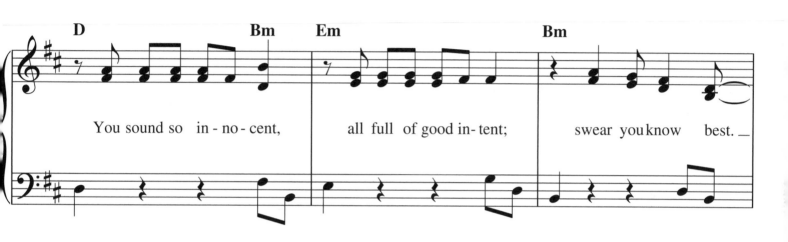

You sound so in-no-cent, all full of good in-tent; swear you know best. _

_ But you ex pect me to jump up on board with you and ride

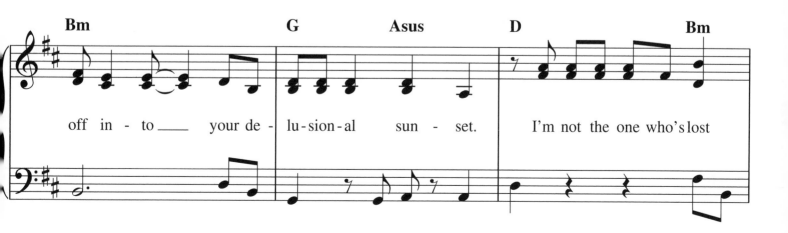

off in-to ___ your de-lu-sion-al sun-set. I'm not the one who's lost

54

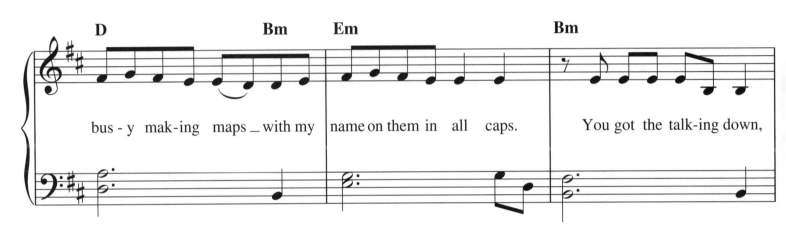

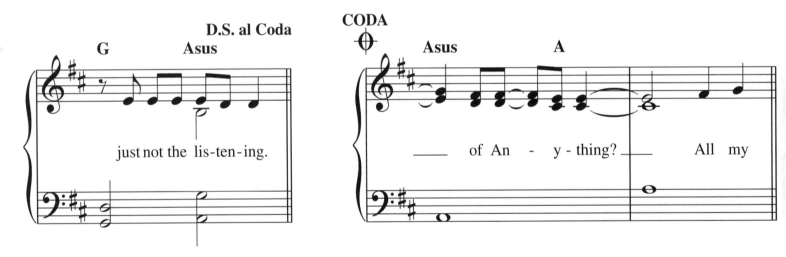

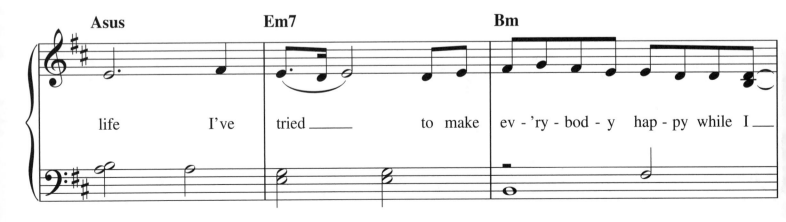

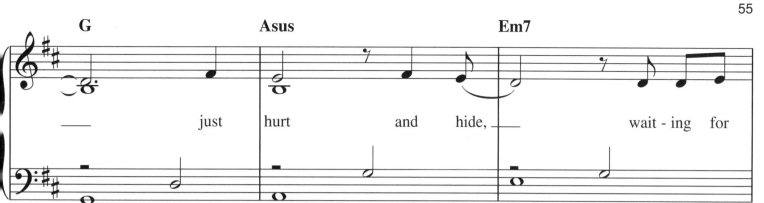

just hurt and hide, ___ wait - ing for

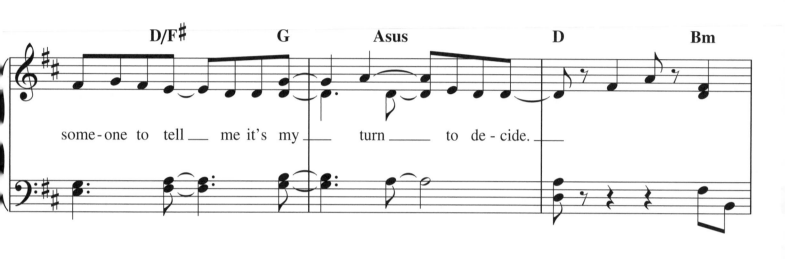

some - one to tell __ me it's my ___ turn ___ to de - cide. ___

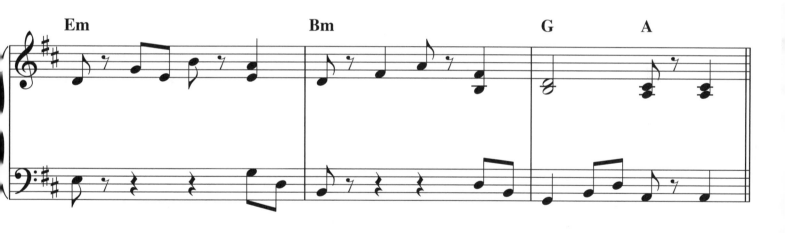

Who cares __ if you dis - a - gree? You are not __ me. Who made you King __

POKER FACE

Words and Music by STEFANI GERMANOTTA
and RedOne

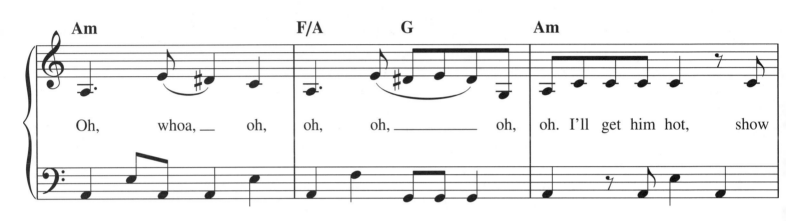

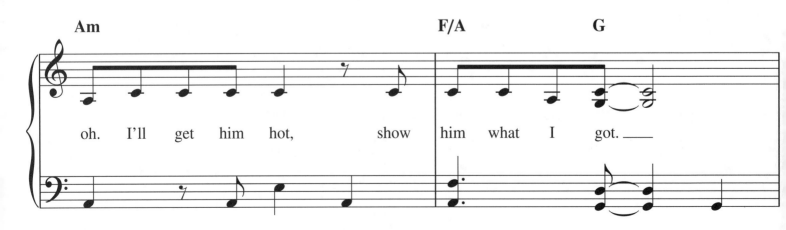

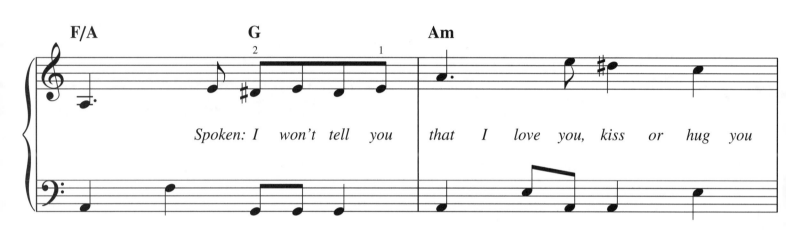

Spoken: I won't tell you that I love you, kiss or hug you

'cause I'm bluf - fin' with my muf - fin. I'm not ly - in', I'm just stun - nin'

with my love glue - gun - nin'. Just like a chick in the ca - si - no,

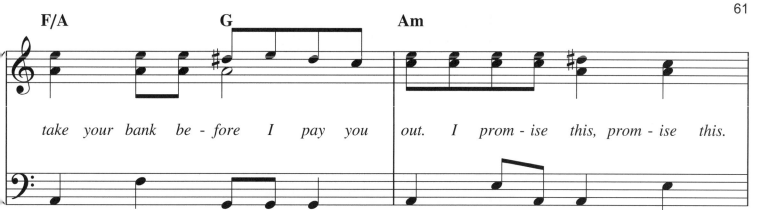

take your bank be - fore I pay you out. I prom - ise this, prom - ise this.

Check this hand,'cause I'm mar - vel - ous.

D.S. al Coda
(no repeat)

CODA

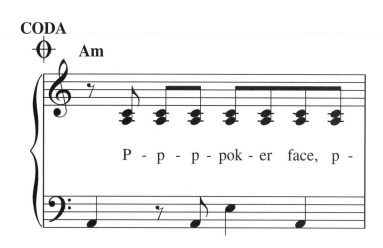

P - p - p - p - pok - er face, p -

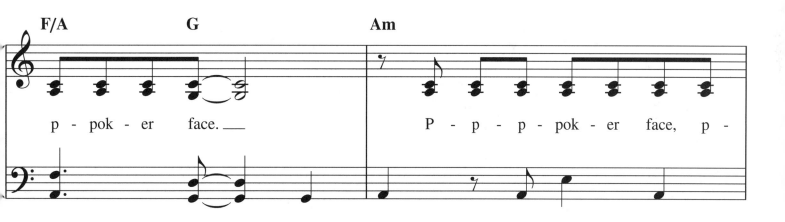

p - pok - er face.___

P - p - p - p - pok - er face, p -

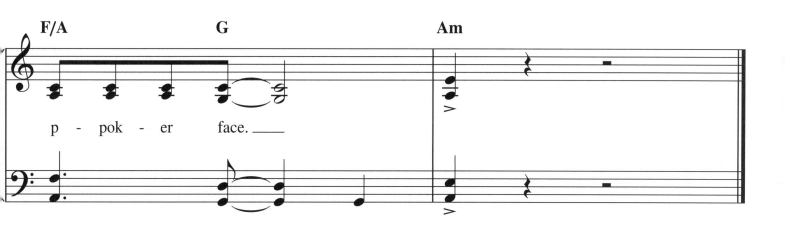

p - pok - er face.___

LOVE SONG

Words and Music by
SARA BAREILLES

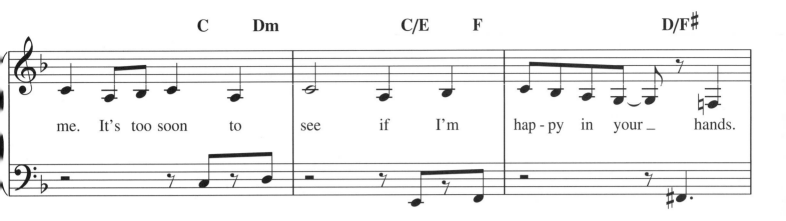

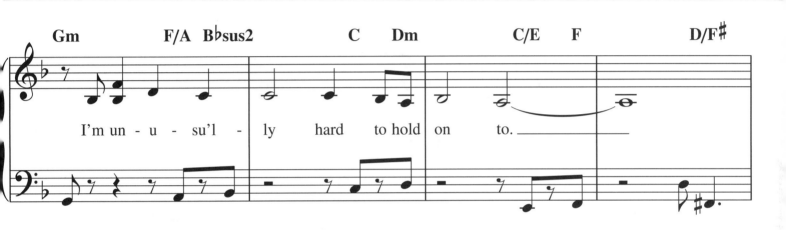

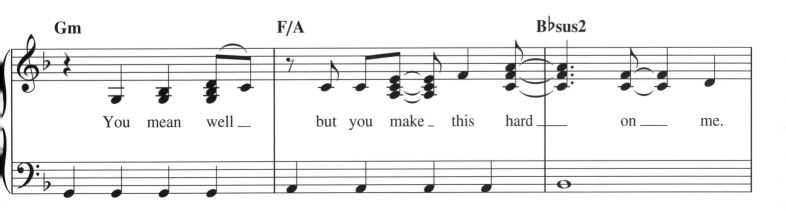

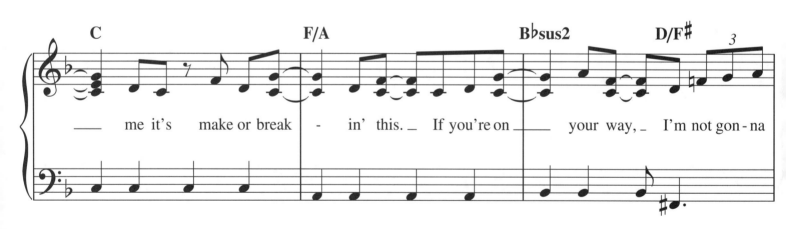

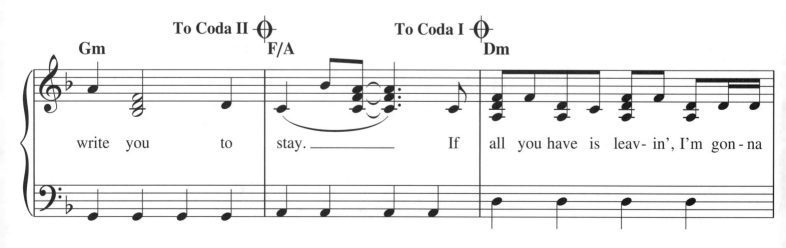

need a bet-ter rea-son to write ___ you ___ a love ___ song to-day, _

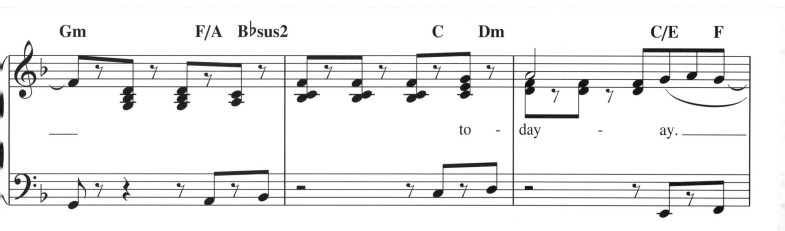

___ to - day - ay. ___

___ I learned the hard way that they all say ___

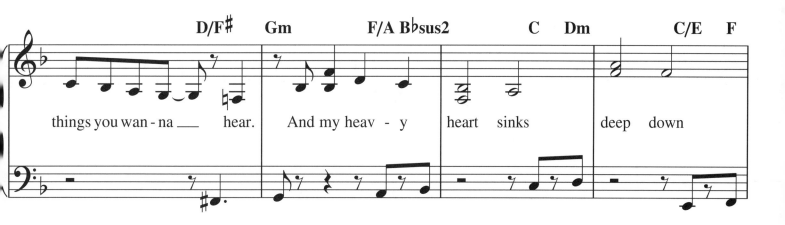

things you wan-na ___ hear. And my heav-y heart sinks deep down

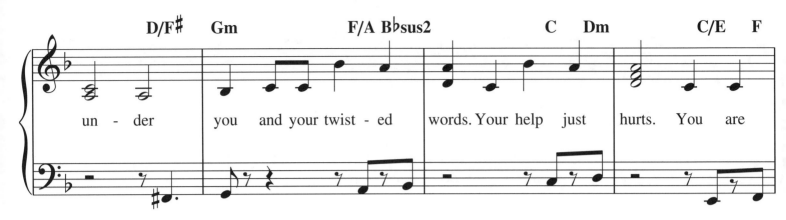

un - der   you   and your twist - ed   words. Your help just   hurts.   You   are

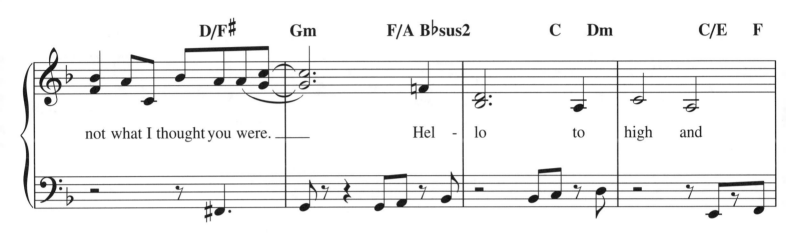

not what I thought you were. ____   Hel - lo   to   high   and

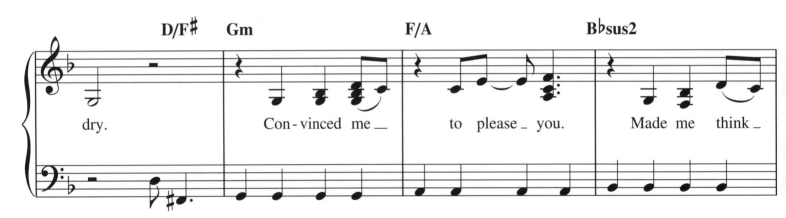

dry.   Con - vinced me __   to   please __ you.   Made me   think __

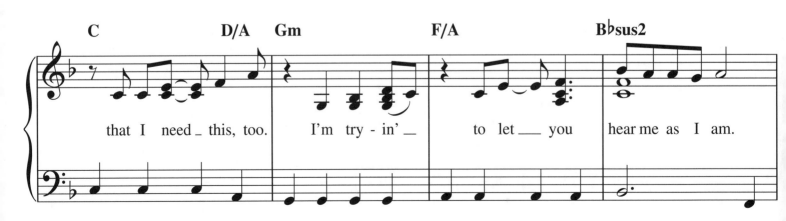

that I need __ this, too.   I'm try - in' __   to   let ___ you   hear me as I am.

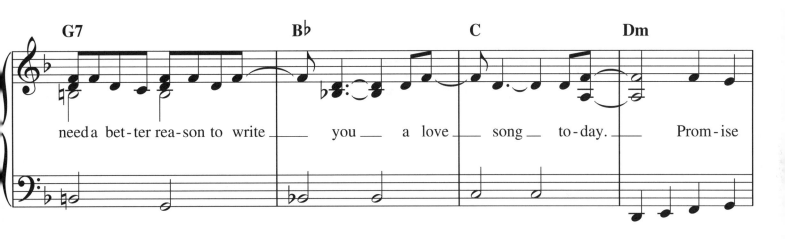

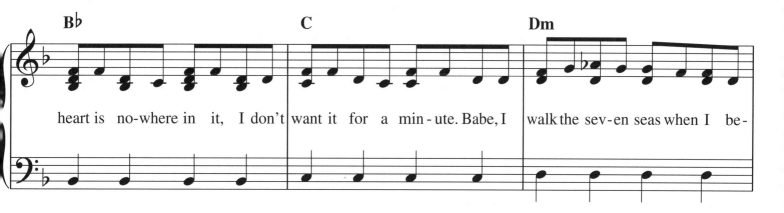

heart is no-where in it, I don't want it for a min-ute. Babe, I walk the sev-en seas when I be-

lieve that there's a rea-son to write you _____ a love _____ song _____ to-day, _____

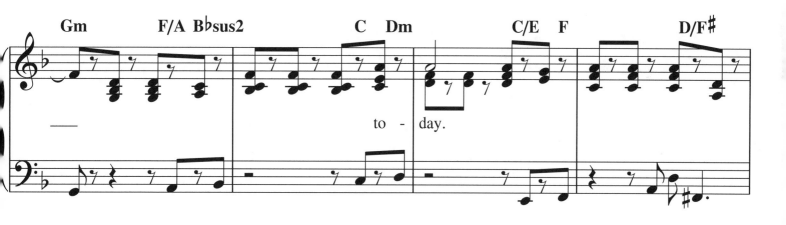

_____ to - day.

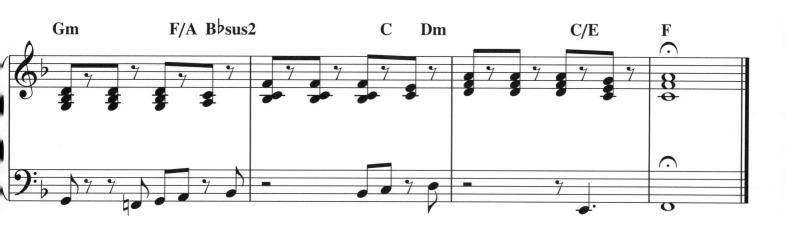

MY LIFE WOULD SUCK WITHOUT YOU

Words and Music by LUKASZ GOTTWALD,
MAX MARTIN and CLAUDE KELLY

Up-beat Pop

Guess this means___ you're
May - be I_____ was

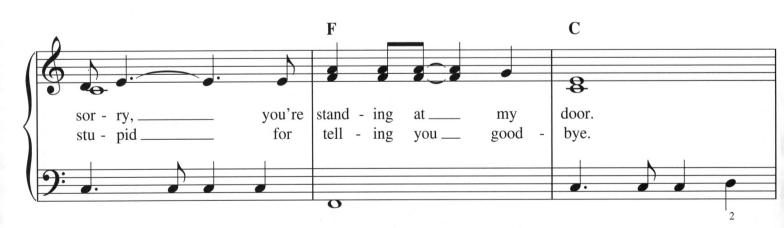

sor - ry,_____ you're stand - ing at___ my door.
stu - pid_____ for tell - ing you___ good - bye.

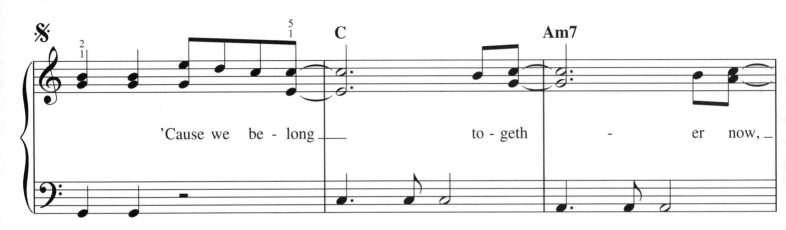

'Cause we be - long _____ to - geth _____ er now, __

__ yeah, for - ev - er u - nit _____ ed here __

__ some-how, __ yeah. You got a piece __ of

me. And hon - est - ly, my

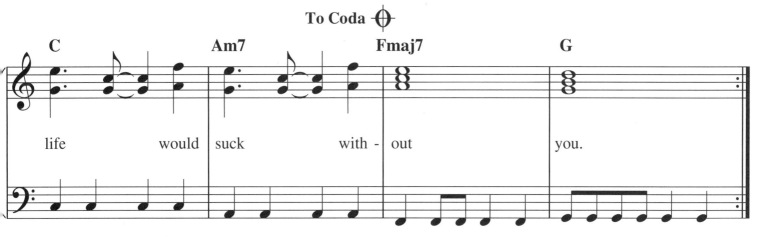

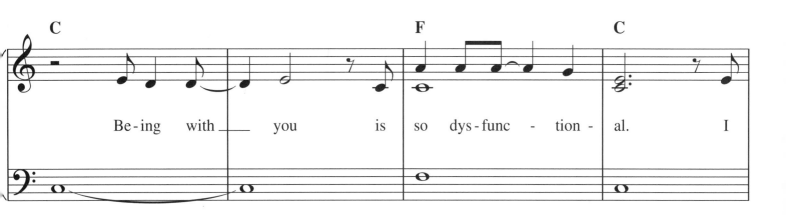

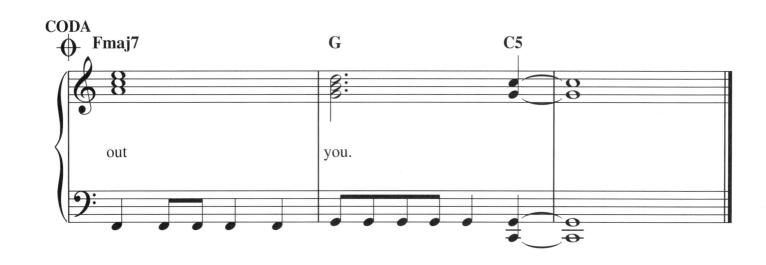

PART OF ME

Words and Music by KATY PERRY,
LUKASZ GOTTWALD, MAX MARTIN
and BONNIE McKEE

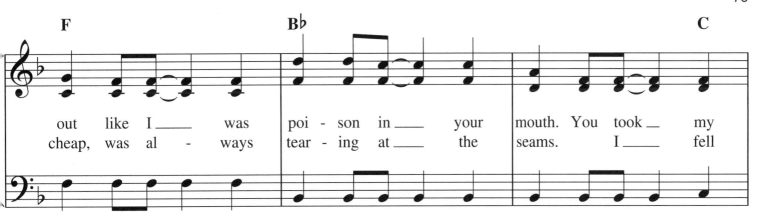

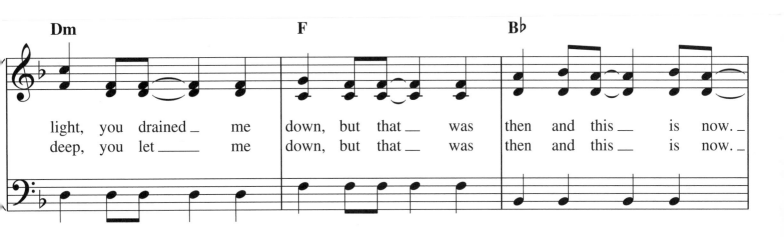

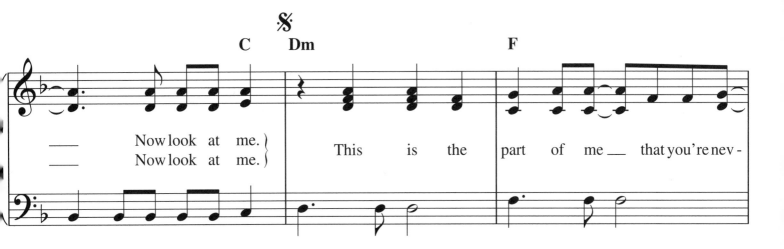

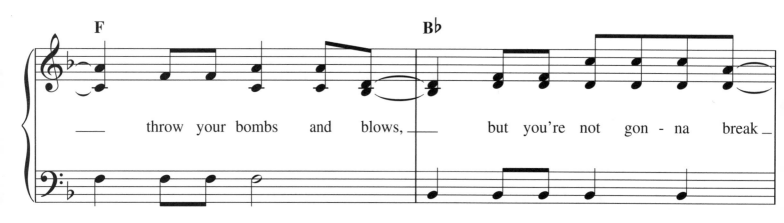

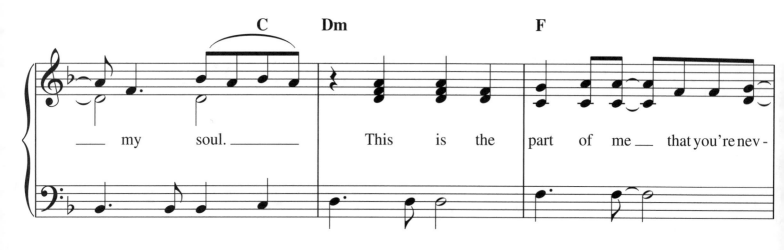

- er gon-na ev - er take a - way from _ me, __ no. | way from _ me, __ no.

Now look at me, I'm spar - kl - ing, __ a

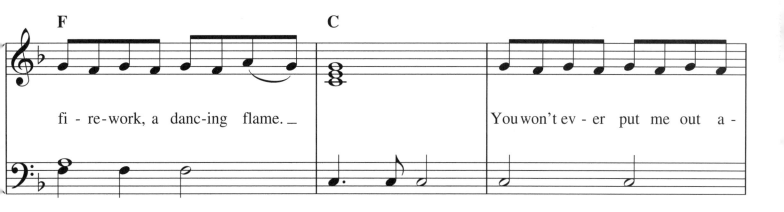

fi - re-work, a danc-ing flame. _ You won't ev - er put me out a -

gain. I'm _ glow - ing, oh. _____ So

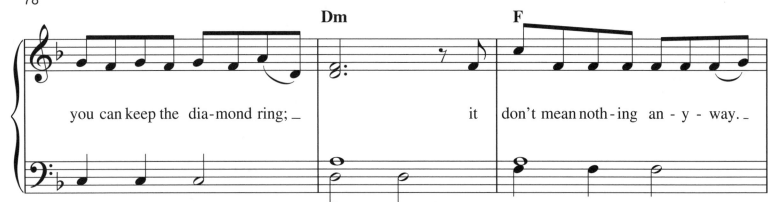

you can keep the dia-mond ring; _ it don't mean noth-ing an-y-way. _

In fact, you can keep ev-'ry-thing, _ yeah, yeah,

ex-cept for me.

way from me, _ no. This is the

part of me, _ no. _

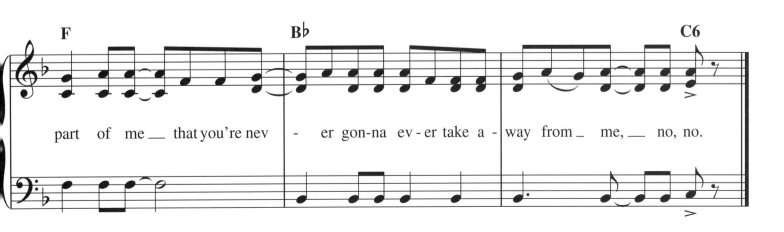

RAISE YOUR GLASS

Words and Music by ALECIA MOORE,
MAX MARTIN and JOHAN SCHUSTER

Right, right, turn off the lights; we gon-na lose our minds to-night.
Slam, slam, oh, hot ___ damn, what part of "par-ty" don't you un-der-stand?

What's the deal-i-o? ___
Wish you'd just ___ freak out. ___

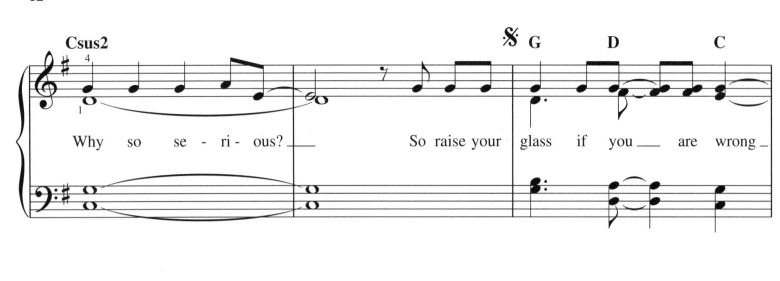

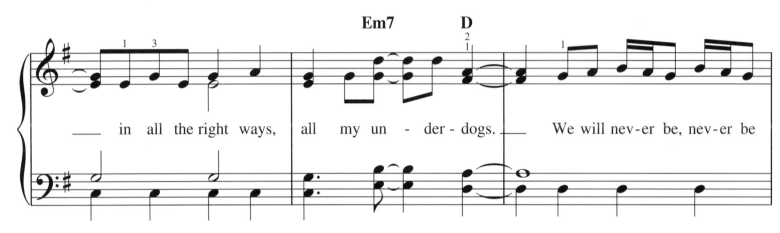

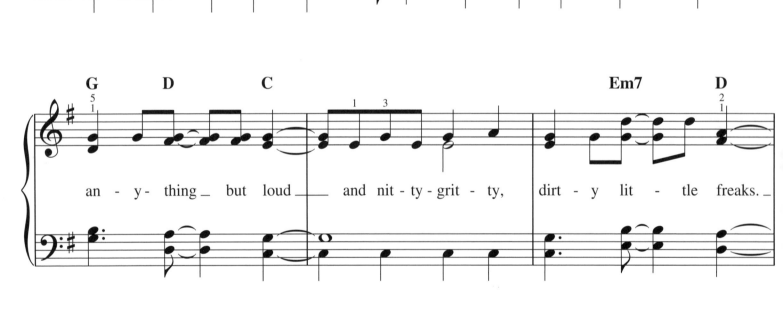

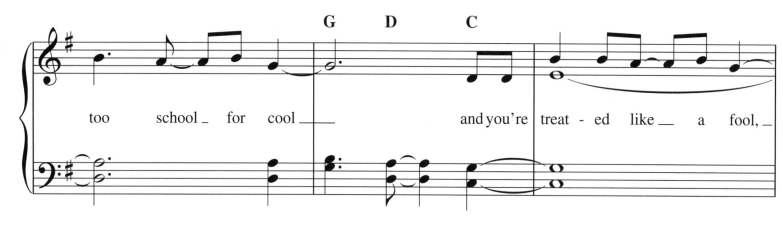

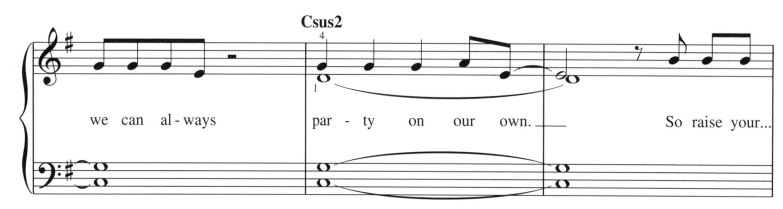

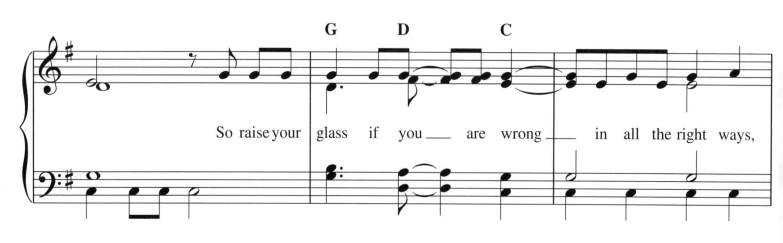

SINGLE LADIES
(Put a Ring on It)

Words and Music by BEYONCE KNOWLES,
THADDIS HARRELL, CHRISTOPHER STEWART
and TERIUS NASH

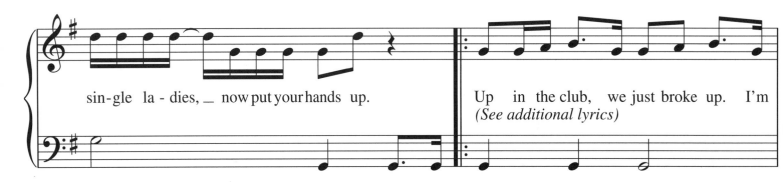

oth - er broth-er no - ticed me.   I'm   up   on   him,   he   up   on   me. Don't

pay   him   an - y   at - ten - tion. _   Just   cried   my   tears   for three good years,   you

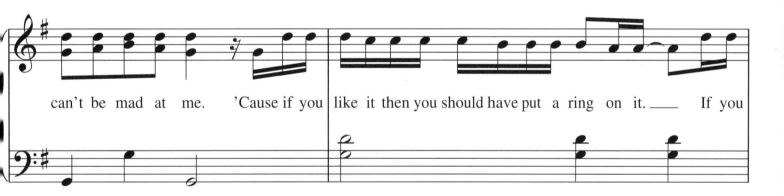

can't be   mad   at   me.   'Cause if you │ like it then you should have put a ring on it. ___   If you

like it then you should have put a ring on it. ___ Don't be │ mad _ once you see _ that he want it. ___ If you

like it then you should have put a ring on it. Oh, oh, oh, oh, oh, oh, oh, ___ oh,

oh, oh, oh, oh. Oh, oh, oh, oh, oh, oh, oh, ___ oh, oh, oh, oh, oh.

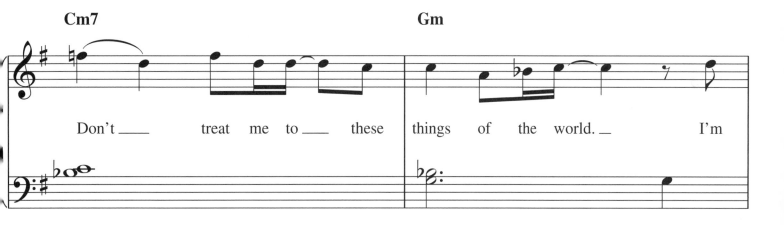

Don't _____ treat me to ____ these things of the world. ___ I'm

not that kind of girl. ___ Your love is what I pre - fer, what I de -

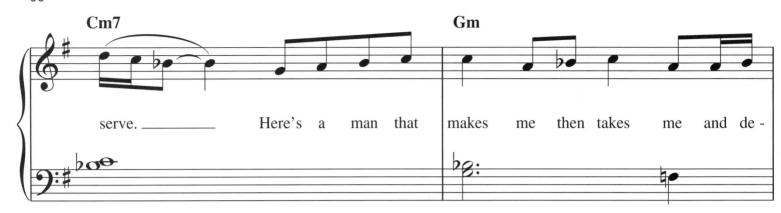

serve. _____ Here's a man that makes me then takes me and de-

liv-ers me ___ to a des-ti-ny, ___ to in-fin-i-ty ___ and be-yond. ___ Pull me

in - to your arms, say I'm the one you want. If you

don't, you'll be a-lone and like a ghost I'll be gone. All the

sin-gle la-dies, _ all the sin-gle la-dies. _ All _ the sin-gle la-dies, _ all the sin-gle la-dies. _ All _ the

sin-gle la-dies, _ all the sin-gle la-dies. _ All _ the sin-gle la-dies, _ now put your hands up. Oh, oh,

oh, oh, oh, oh, oh, _ oh, oh, oh, oh, oh. Oh, oh, oh, oh, oh, oh, oh, _ oh,

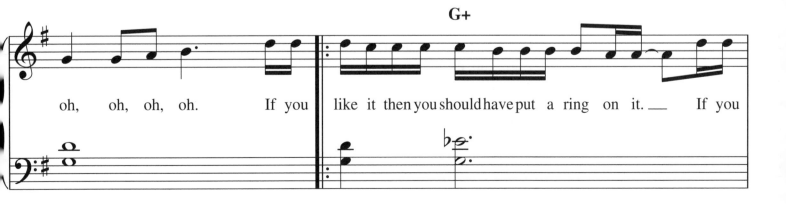

oh, oh, oh, oh. If you like it then you should have put a ring on it. _ If you

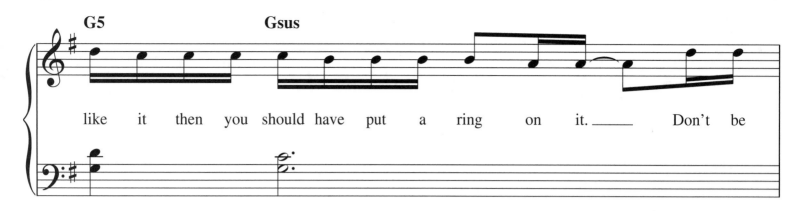

Additional Lyrics

I got gloss on my lips, a man on my hips,
Hold me tighter than my Dereon jeans.
Actin' up, drink in my cup,
I can care less what you think.
I need no permission. Did I mention?
Don't pay him any attention.
'Cause you had your turn and now you gon' learn
What it really feels like to miss me.

STRONGER
(What Doesn't Kill You)

Words and Music by GREG KURSTIN,
JORGEN ELOFSSON, DAVID GAMSON
and ALEXANDRA TAMPOSI

Moderate Dance groove

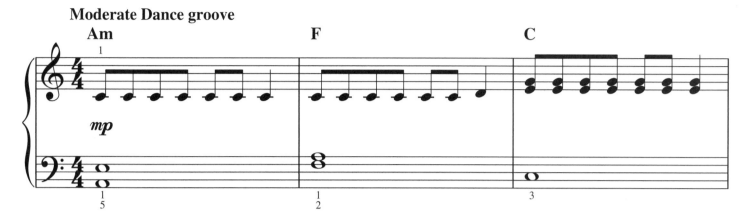

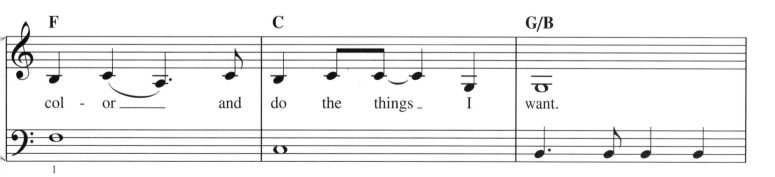

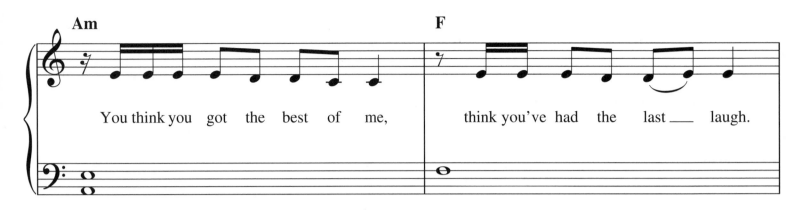

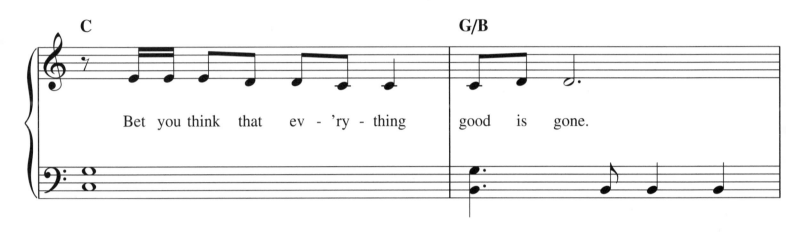

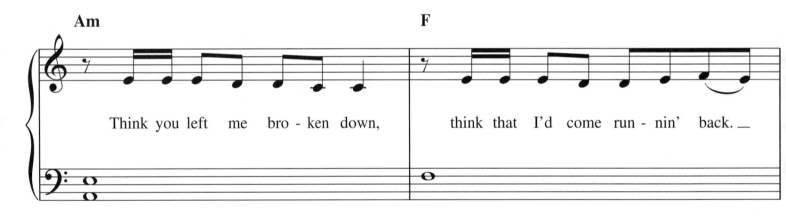

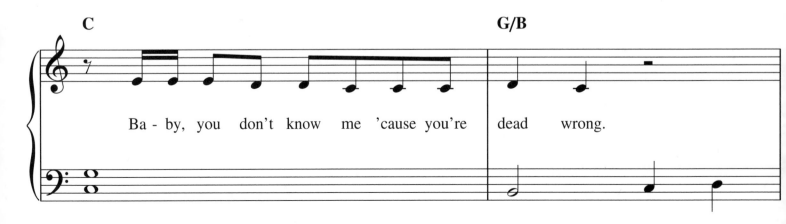

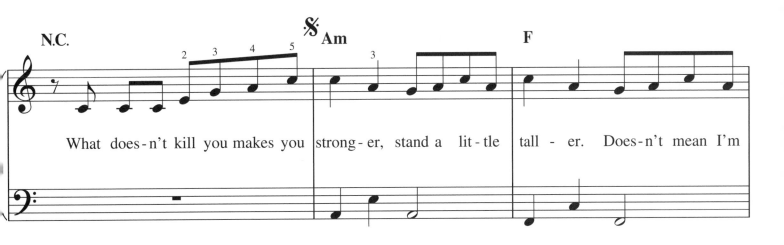

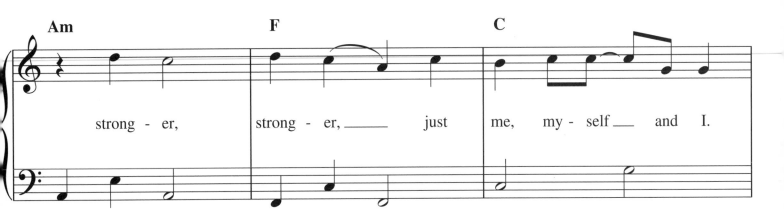

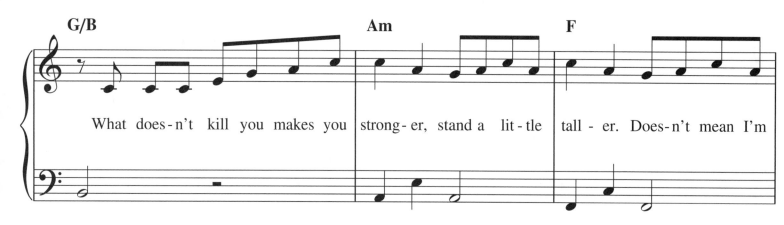

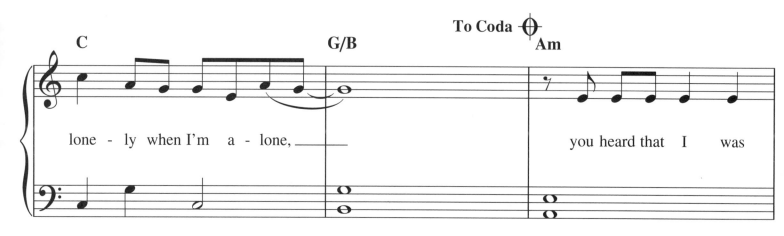

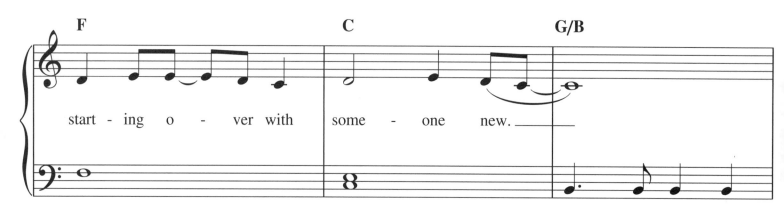

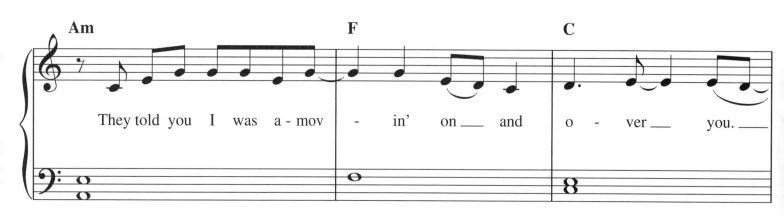

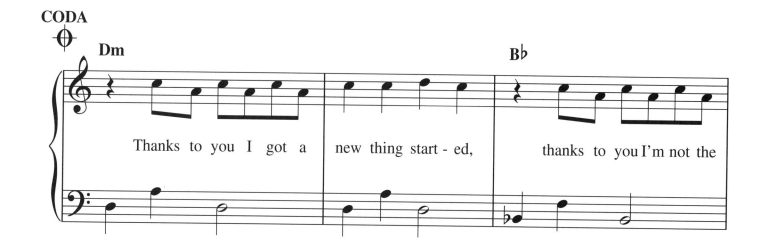

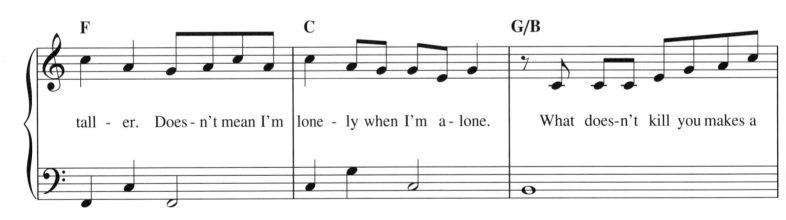

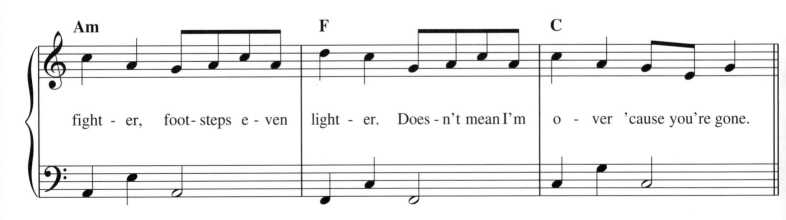

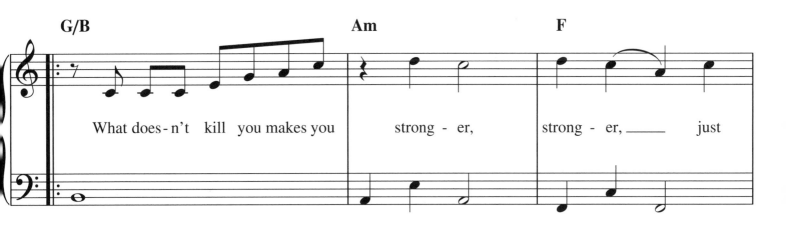

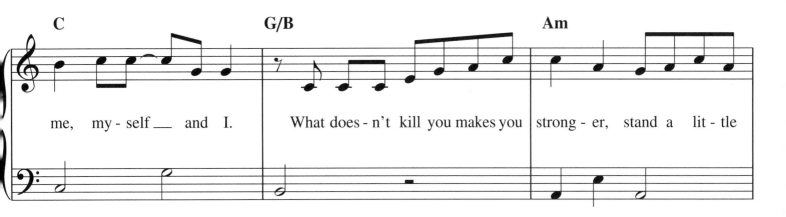

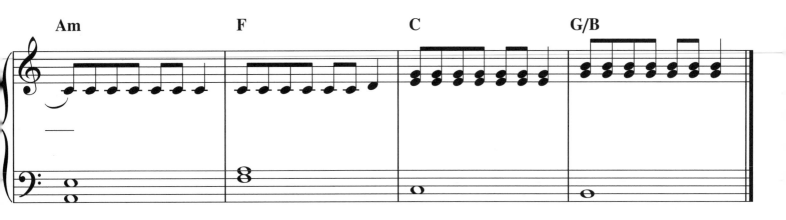

SKYFALL
from the Motion Picture SKYFALL

Words and Music by ADELE ADKINS
and PAUL EPWORTH

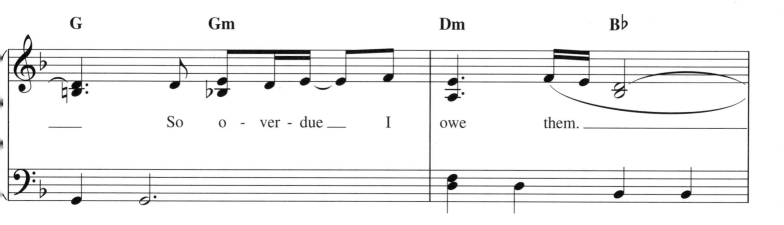

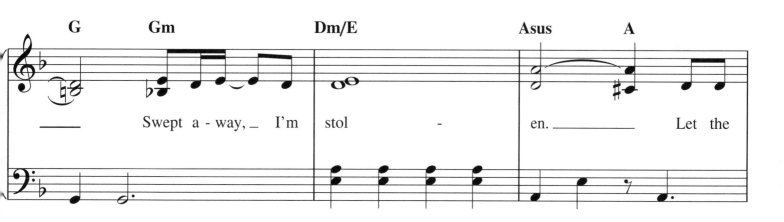

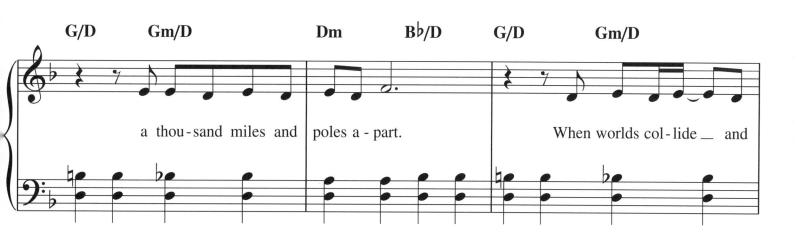

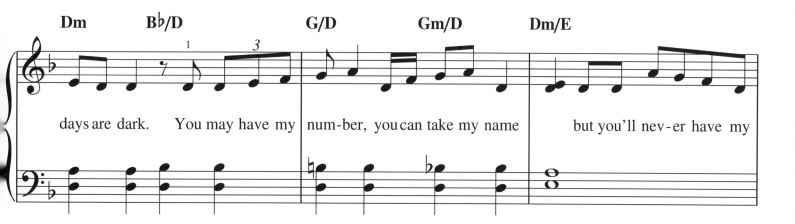

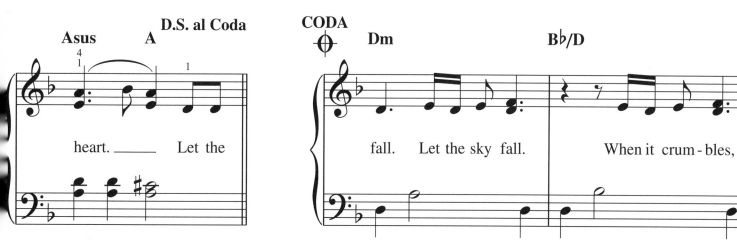

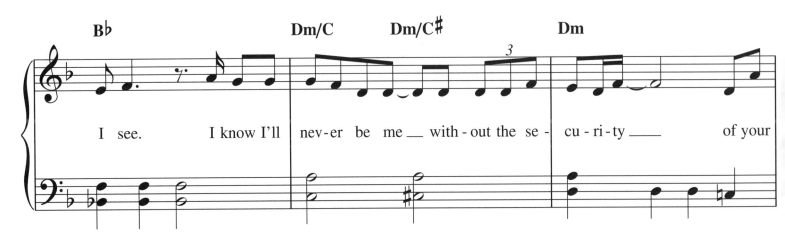

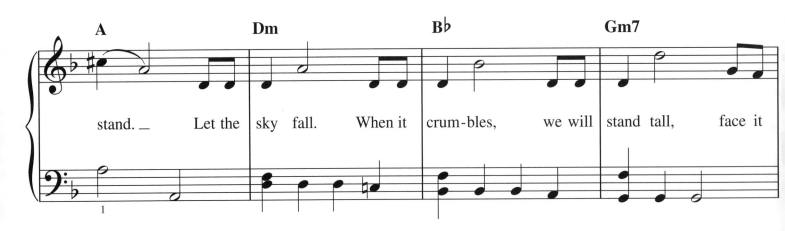

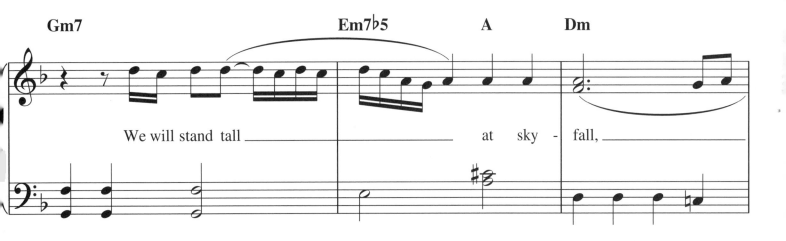

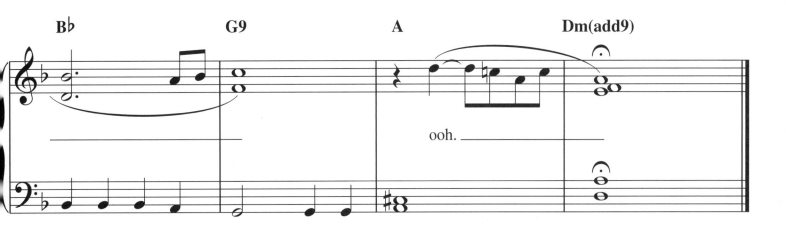

SOMEONE LIKE YOU

Words and Music by ADELE ADKINS
and DAN WILSON

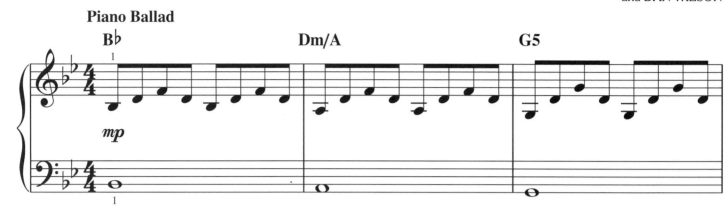

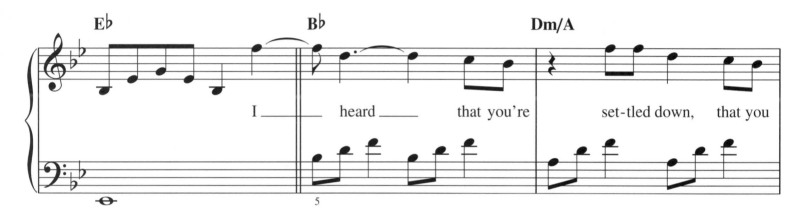

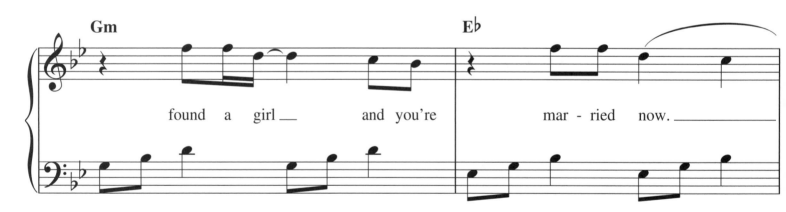

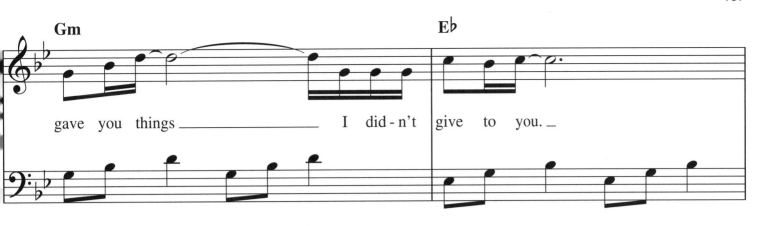

gave you things _____ I did‑n't give to you. __

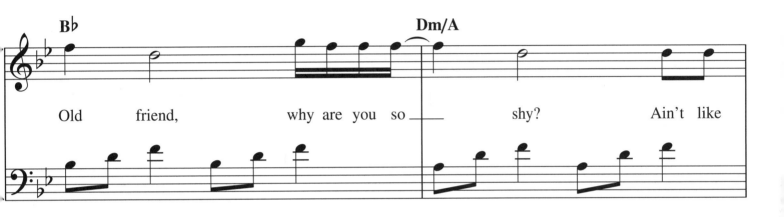

Old friend, why are you so ___ shy? Ain't like

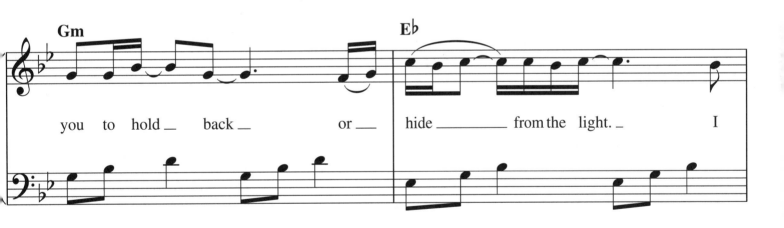

you to hold __ back __ or __ hide _____ from the light. __ I

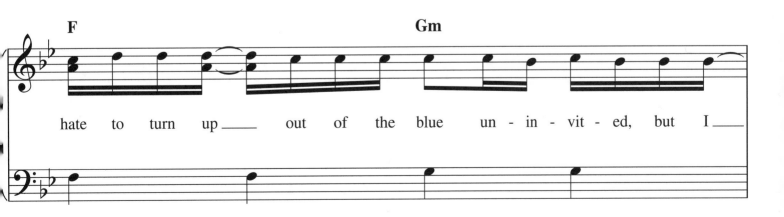

hate to turn up ____ out of the blue un‑in‑vit‑ed, but I ____

could - n't stay a - way, ____ I could - n't fight it. I had

hoped you'd see my face and that you'd be re - mind - ed that, for

me, ____ it is - n't o - ver. ____

Nev - er mind, _ I'll find some-one like you. I wish

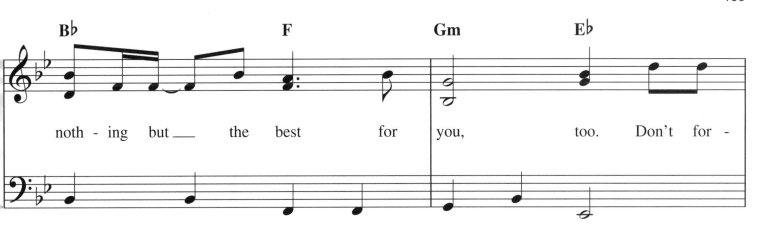

nothing but __ the best for you, too. Don't for-

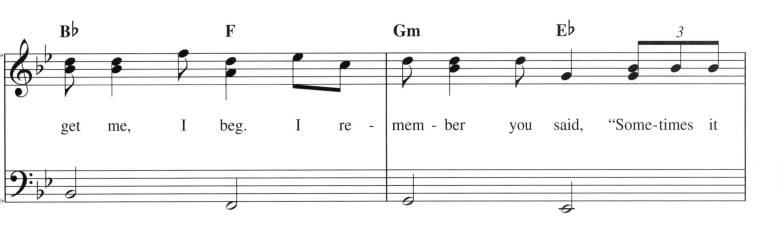

get me, I beg. I re - mem - ber you said, "Some-times it

To Coda ⊕

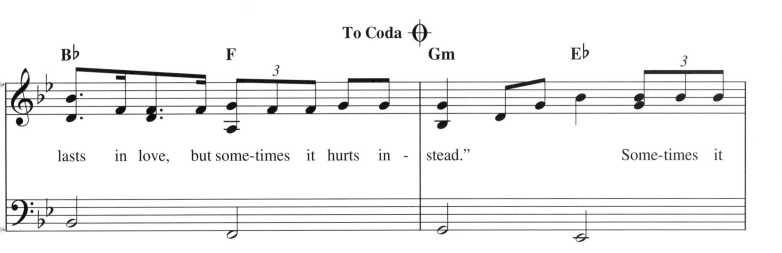

lasts in love, but some-times it hurts in - stead." Some-times it

lasts in love, but some-times it hurts in - stead. _____

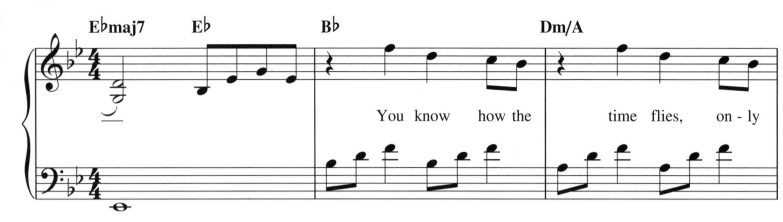

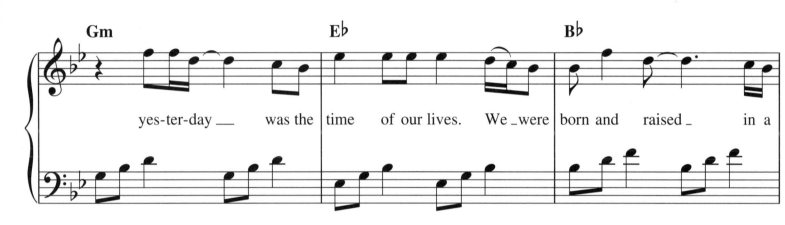

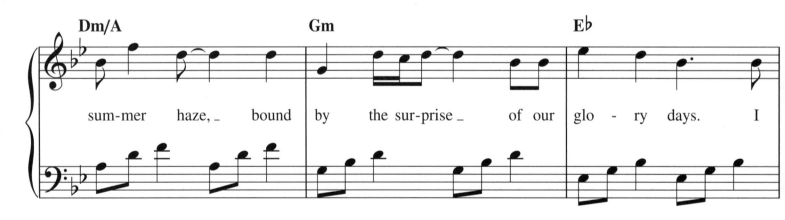

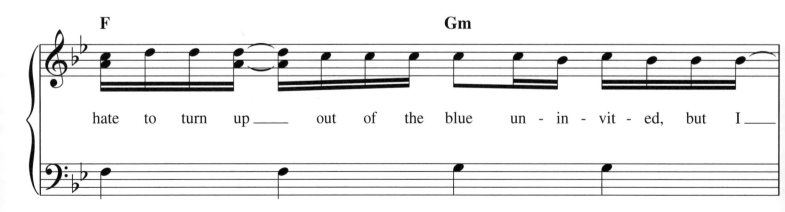

____ could - n't stay a - way, ____ I could - n't fight it. I had

hoped you'd see my face and that you'd be re - mind - ed that, for

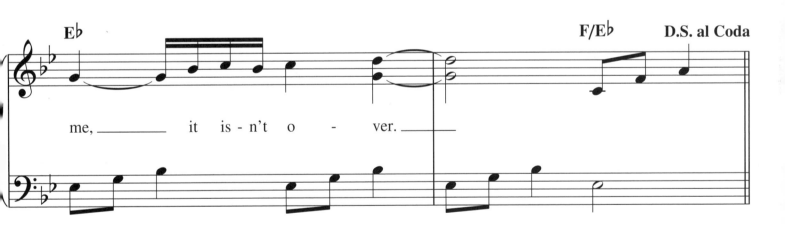

me, _____ it is - n't o - ver. _____

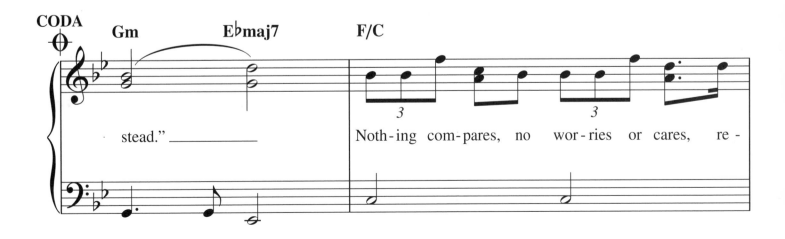

stead." _____ Noth - ing com - pares, no wor - ries or cares, re -

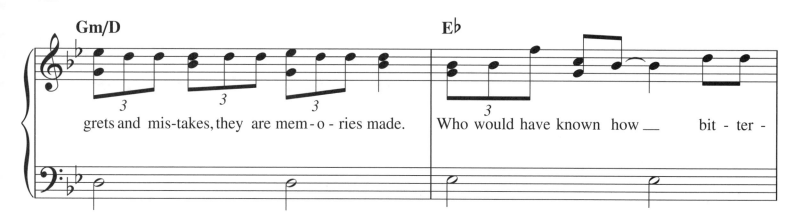

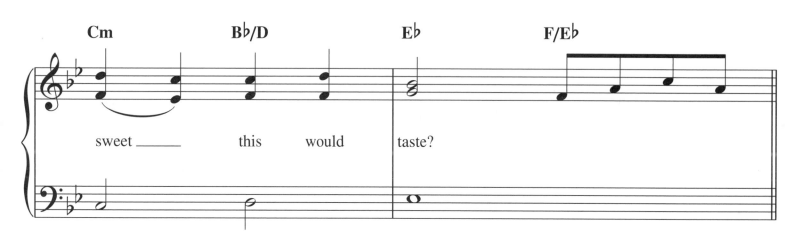

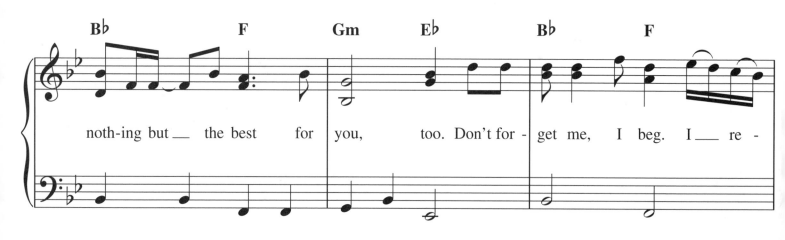

mem - ber   you said, "Some-times it   lasts   in love, but some-times it hurts in -

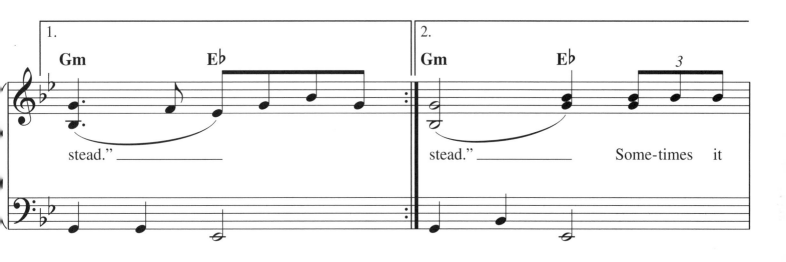

1.
stead." _____

2.
stead." _____   Some-times   it

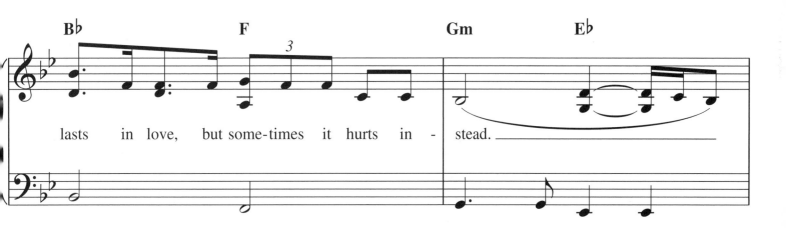

lasts   in love,   but some-times it hurts   in -   stead. _____

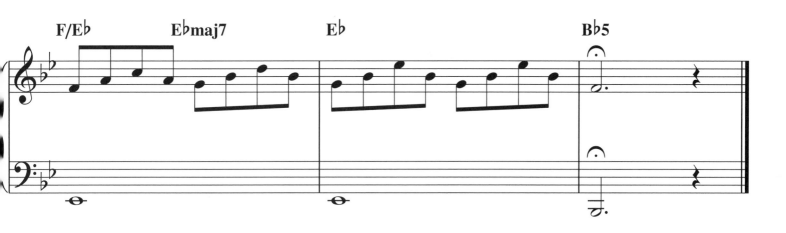

TEENAGE DREAM

Words and Music by KATY PERRY,
BONNIE McKEE, LUKASZ GOTTWALD,
MAX MARTIN and BENJAMIN LEVIN

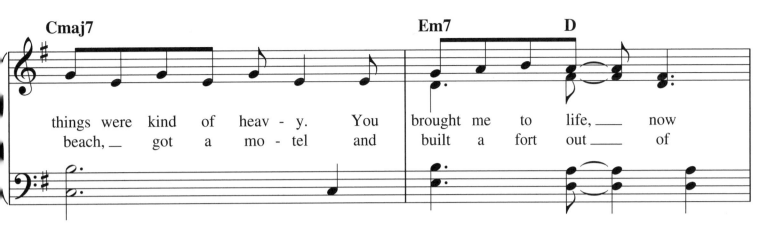

things were kind of heav - y. You
beach, — got a mo - tel and

brought me to life, __ now
built a fort out __ of

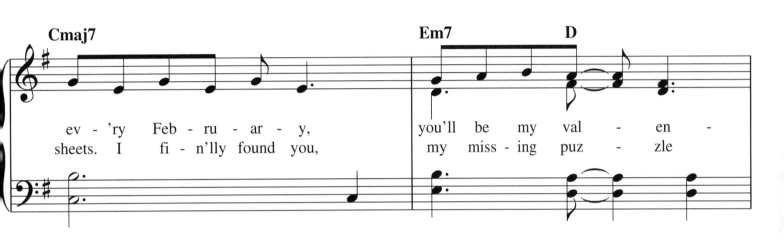

ev - 'ry Feb - ru - ar - y,
sheets. I fi - n'lly found you,

you'll be my val - en -
my miss - ing puz - zle

tine, _____ val - en - tine. ___
piece. _____ I'm com - plete. ___

Let's go all the way __

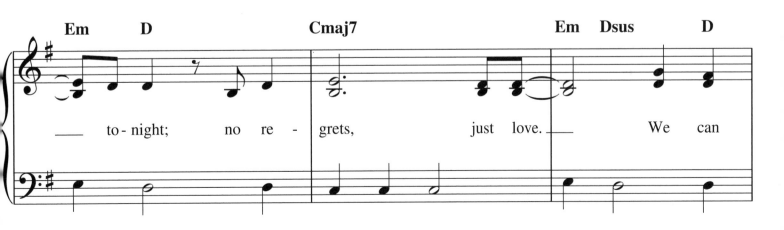

__ to - night; no re - grets, just love. __ We can

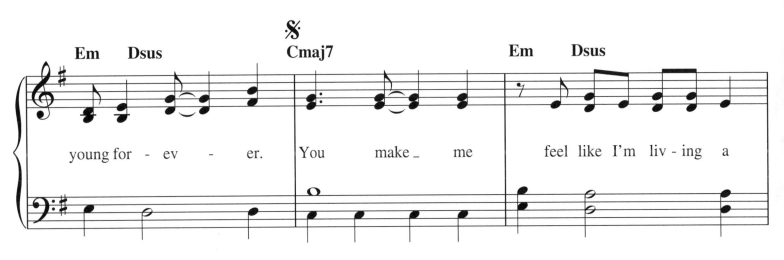

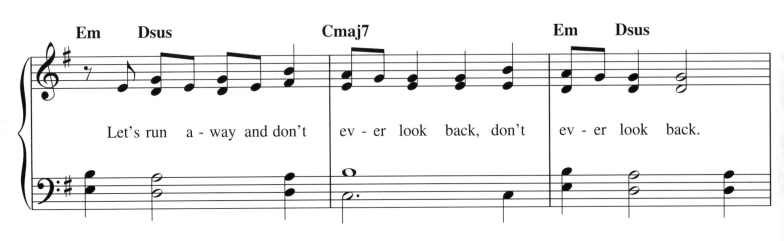

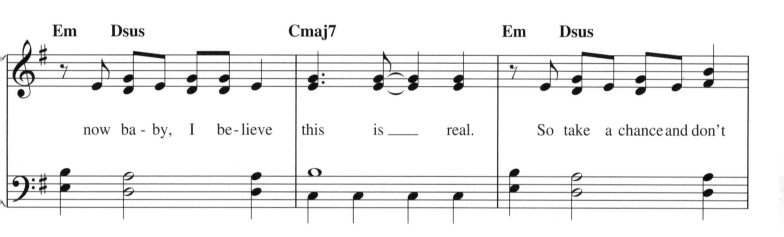

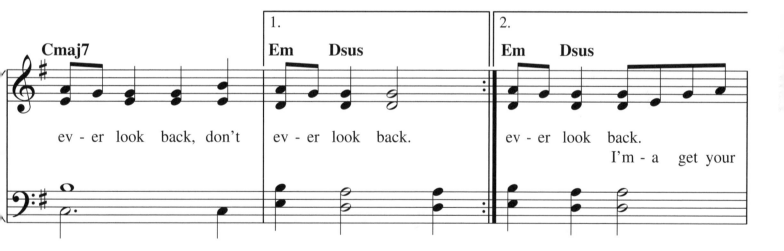

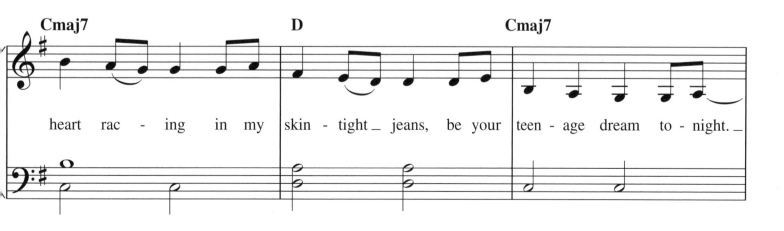

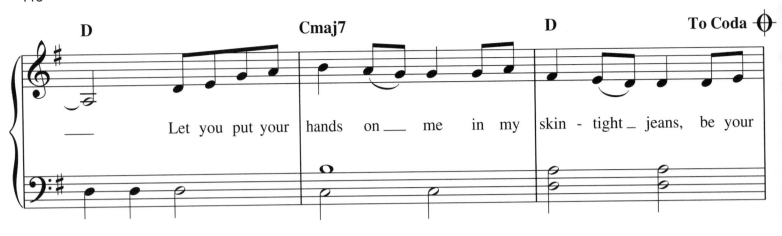

Let you put your hands on ___ me in my skin - tight ___ jeans, be your

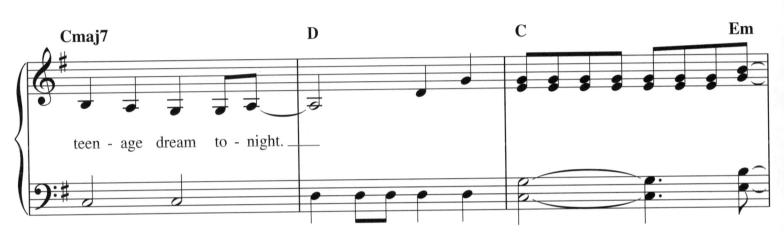

teen - age dream to - night. ___

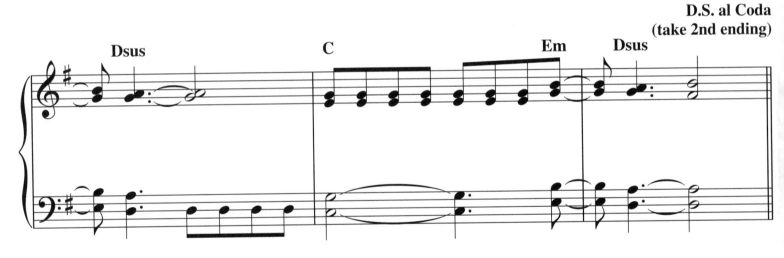

teen - age dream to - night. ___

A THOUSAND MILES

Words and Music by
VANESSA CARLTON

1., 3. Mak-in' my way__ down - town,__ walk - in' fast,__ fac - es pass__

2. (See additional lyrics)

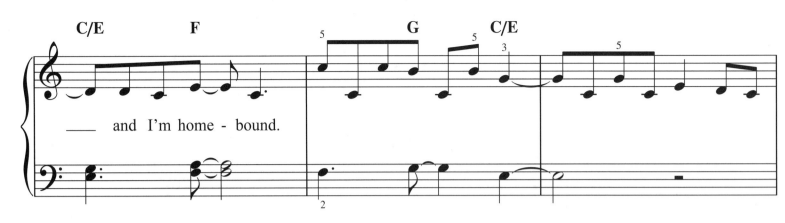

_____ and I'm home - bound.

Star-in' blank - ly a - head,_

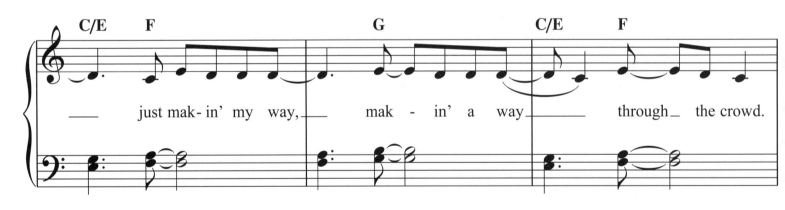

_____ just mak- in' my way,_ mak - in' a way_____ through_ the crowd.

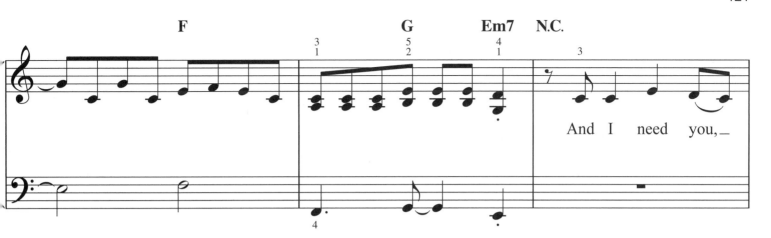

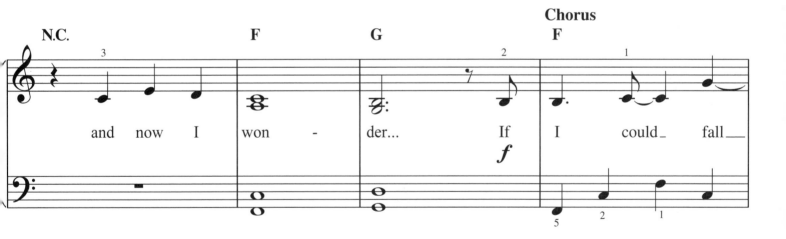

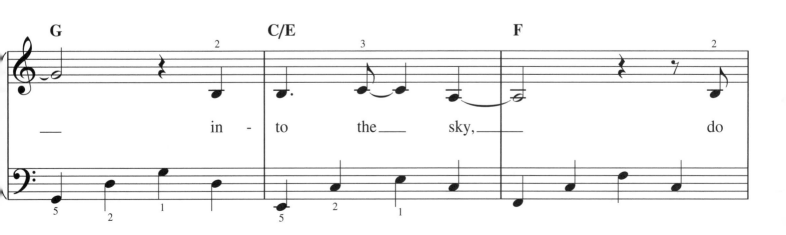

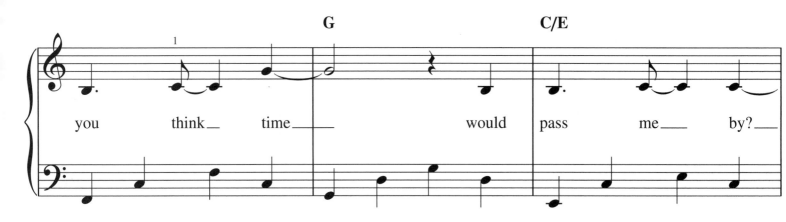

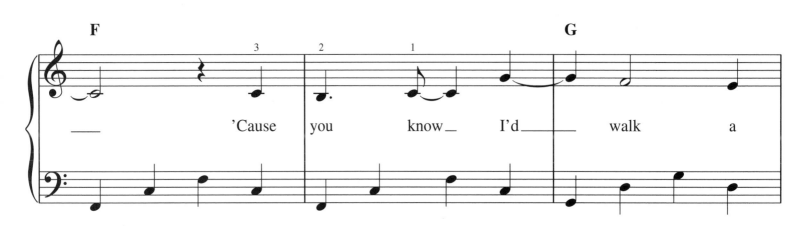

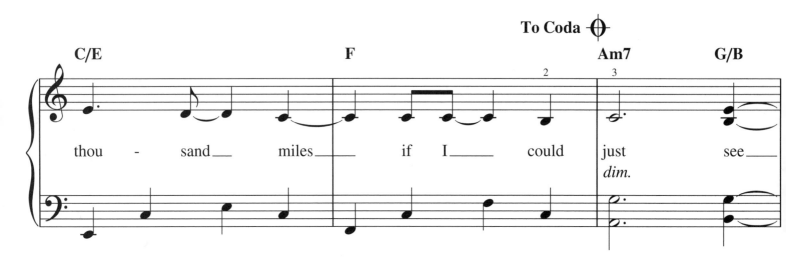

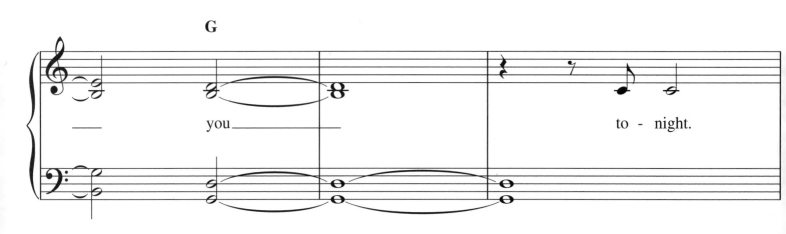

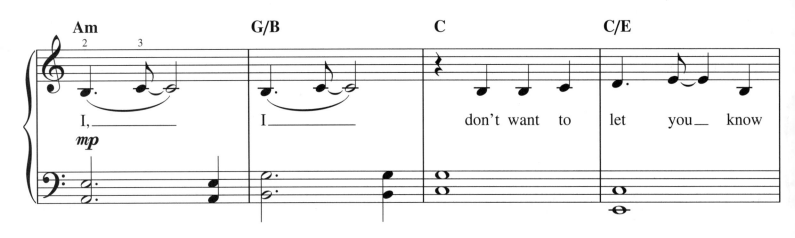

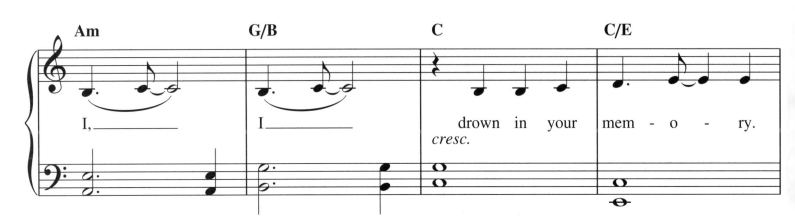

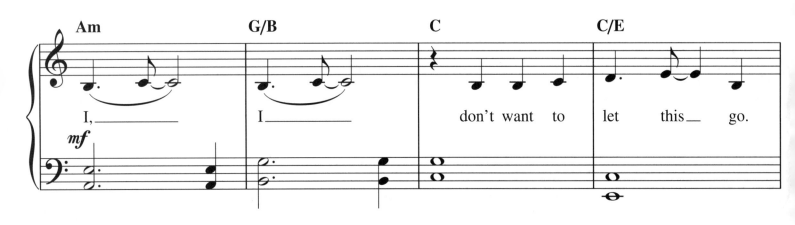

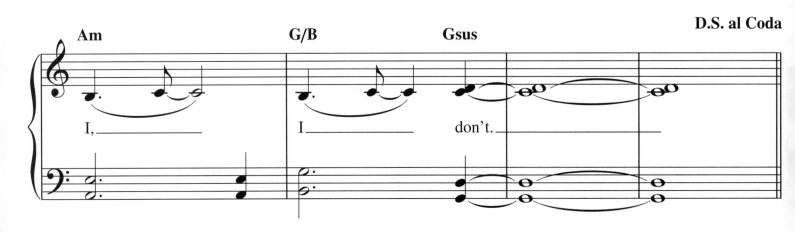

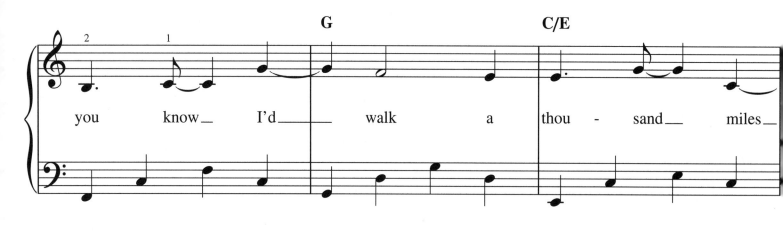

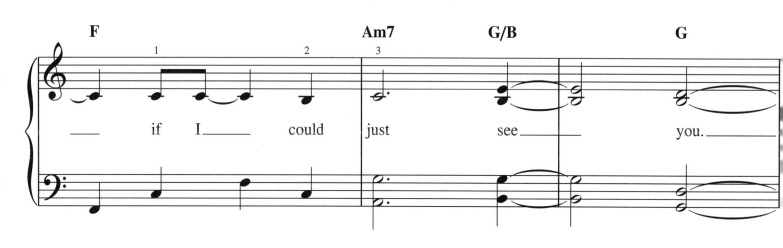

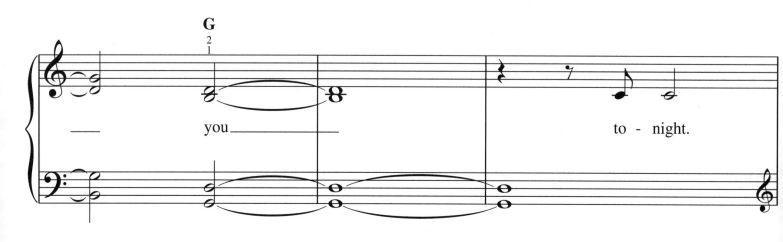

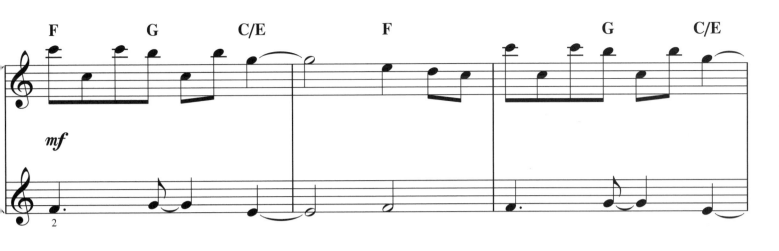

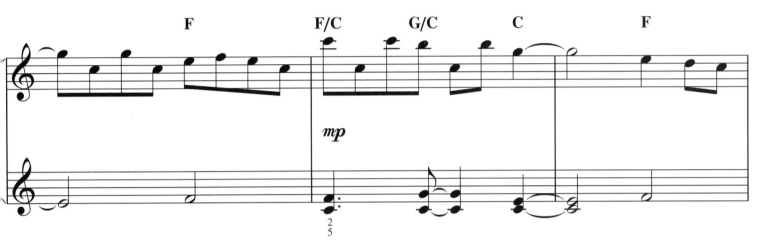

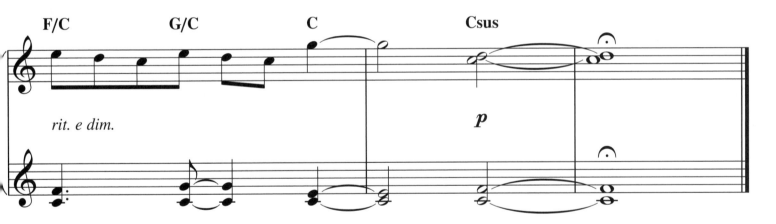

Additional Lyrics

2. It's always times like these when I think of you
   And wonder if you ever think of me.
   'Cause everything's so wrong and I don't belong
   Livin' in your precious memory.
   'Cause I need you,
   And I miss you,
   And I wonder....
   Chorus

A THOUSAND YEARS

from the Summit Entertainment film THE TWILIGHT SAGA: BREAKING DAWN – PART 1

Words and Music by DAVID HODGES
and CHRISTINA PERRI

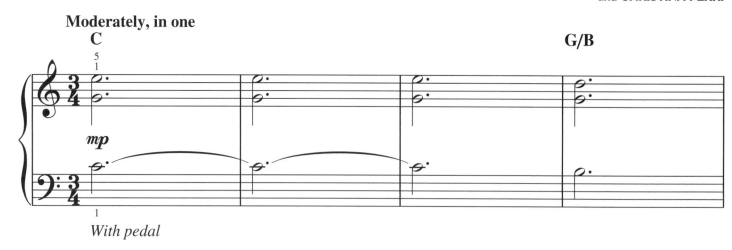

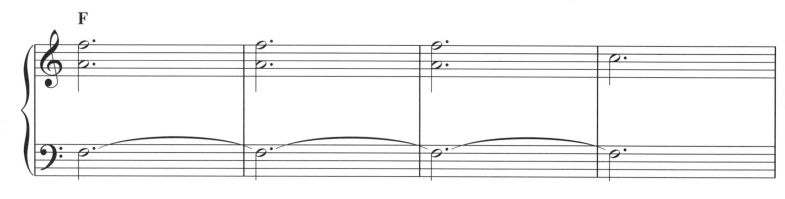

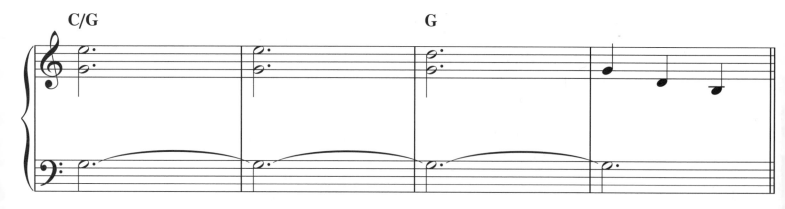

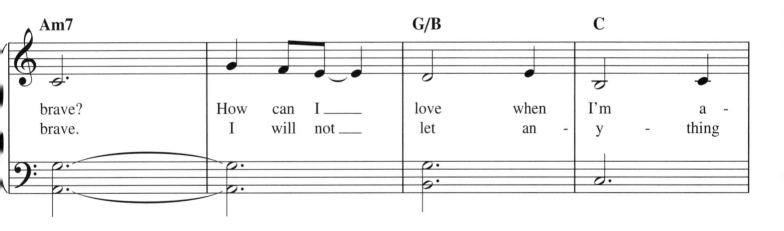

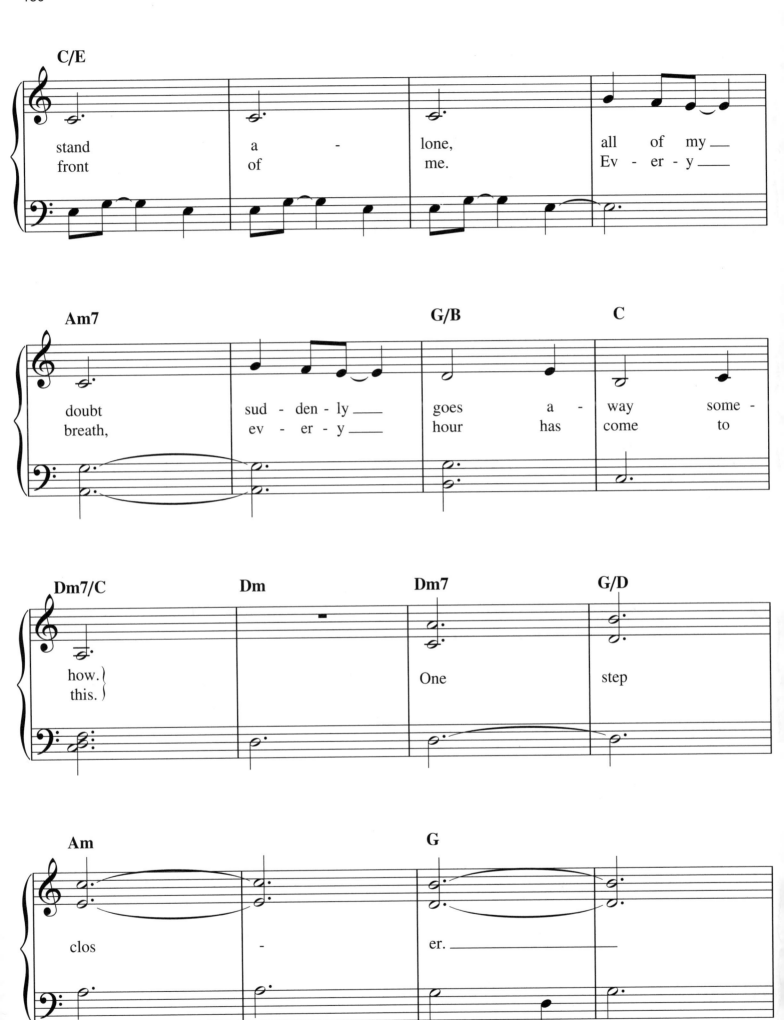

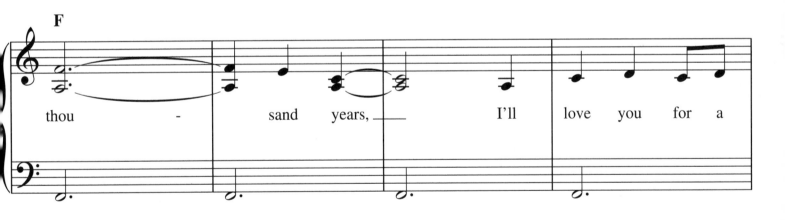

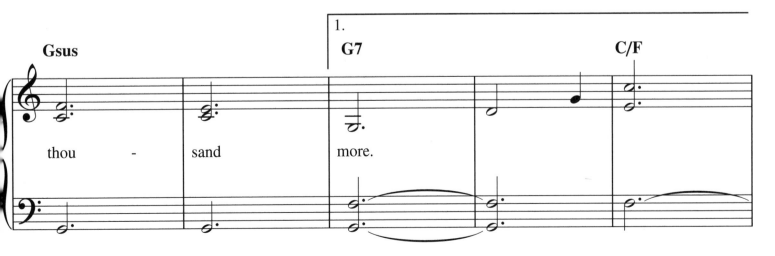

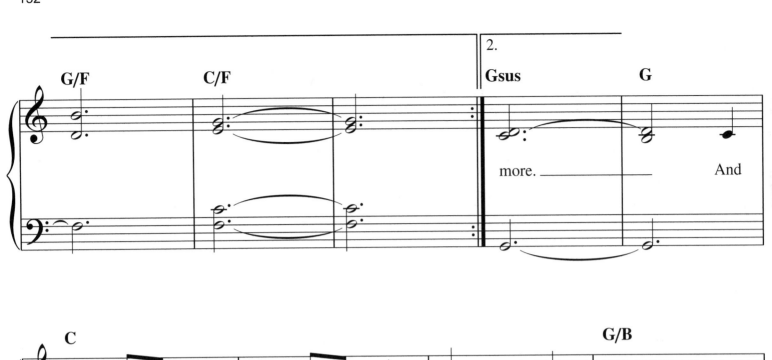

more. _____ And

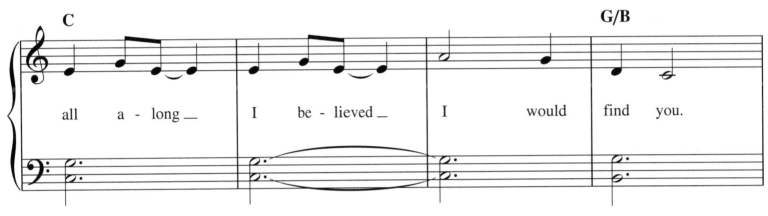

all a - long ___ I be - lieved ___ I would find you.

Time has brought ___ your heart to me; ___ I have loved you for a

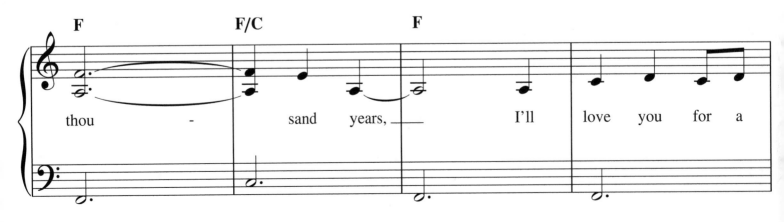

thou - sand years, ___ I'll love you for a

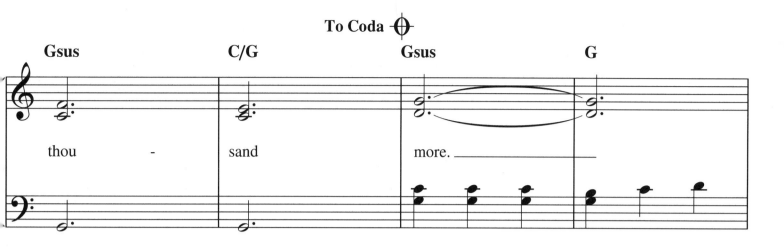

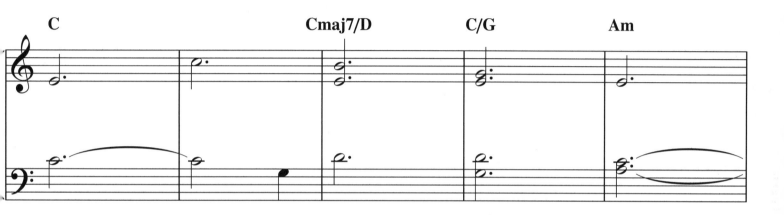

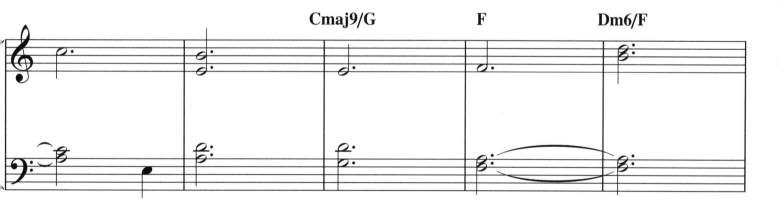

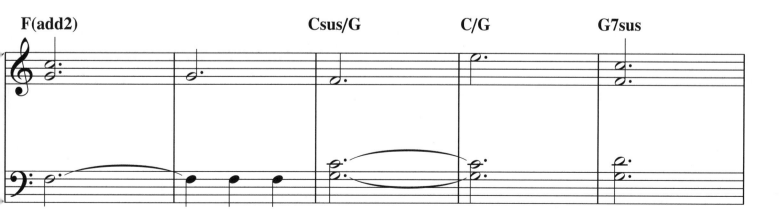

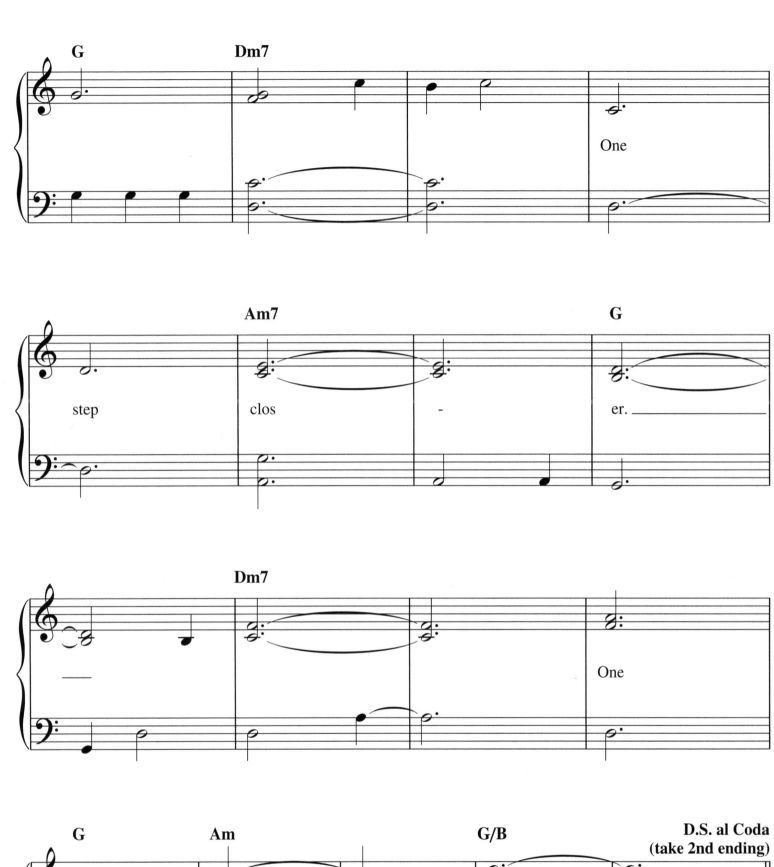

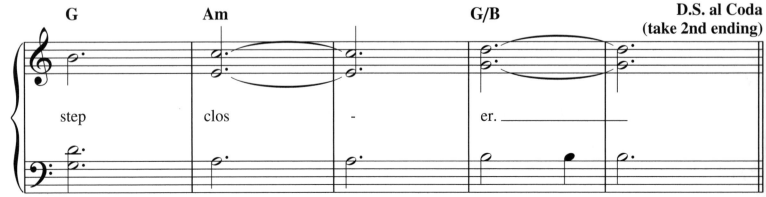

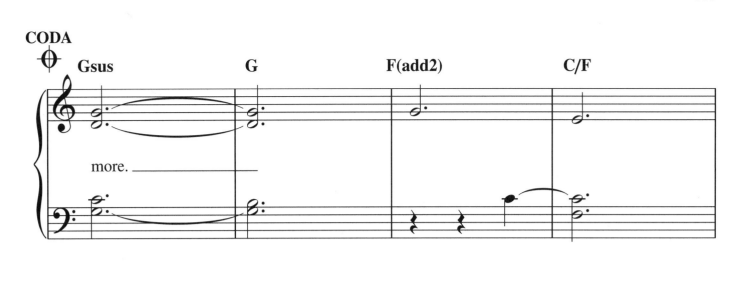

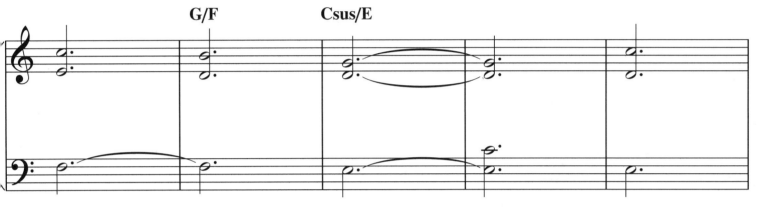

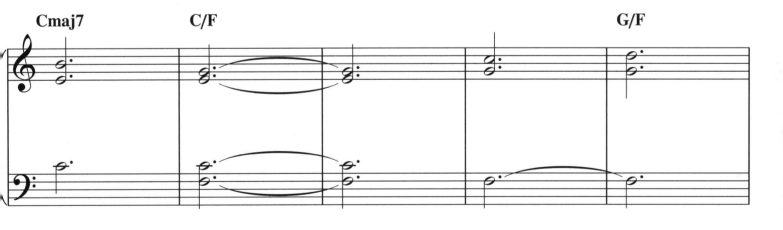

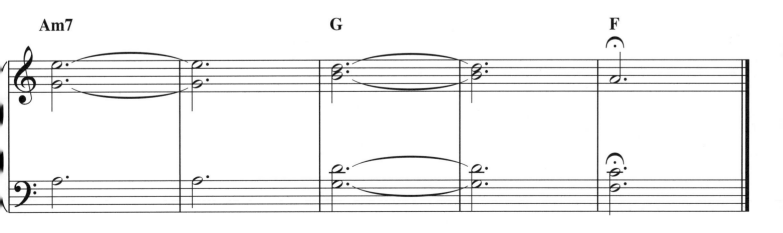

WHITE HOUSES

Words and Music by VANESSA CARLTON
and STEPHAN JENKINS

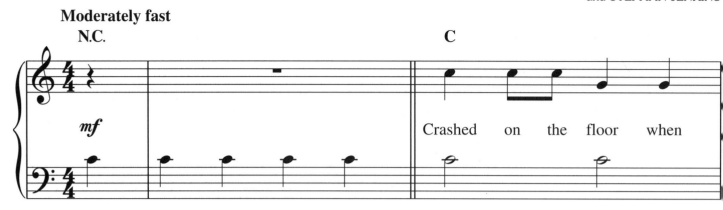

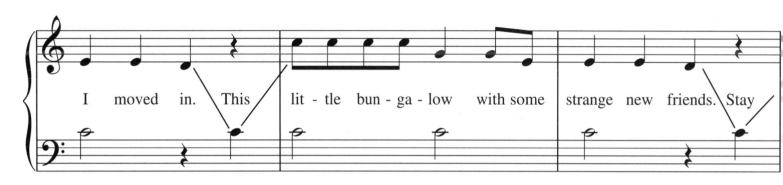

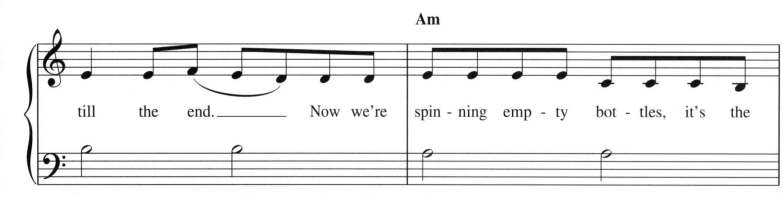

five of us___ with pret - ty - eyed boys girls die to trust.__ I

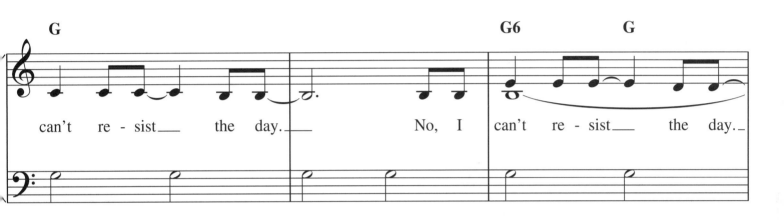

can't re - sist___ the day.___ No, I can't re - sist___ the day.__

___ And Jen - ny screams out and it's no pose, 'cause

when she danc - es she goes and goes. And beer through the nose on an

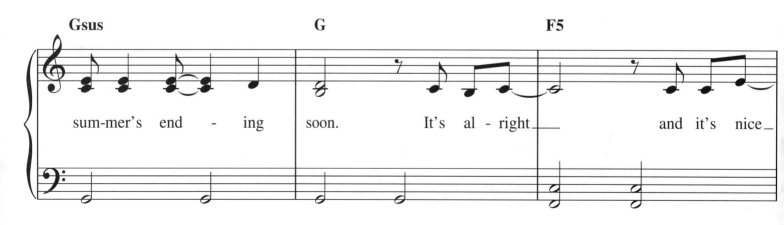

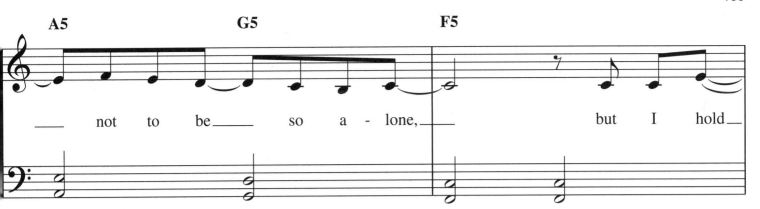

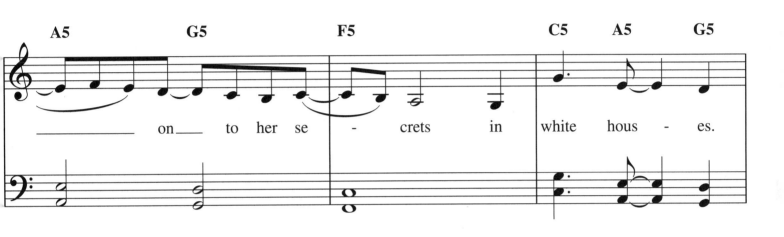

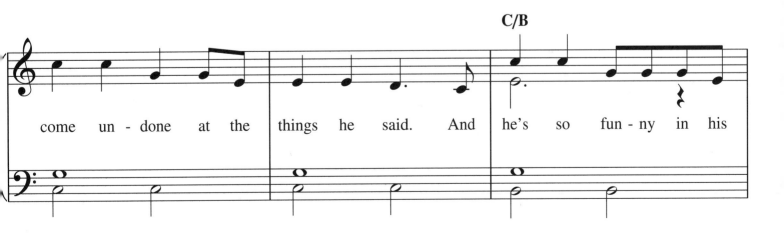

bright red shirt. We were all in love___ and we all got hurt.___ I

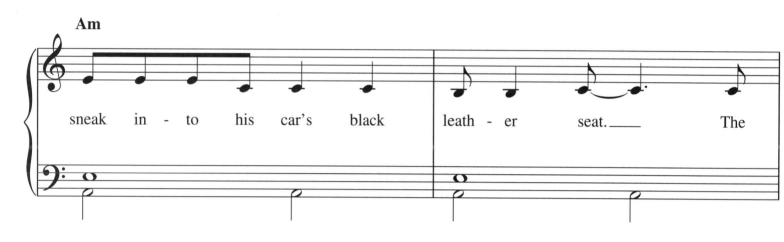

Am

sneak in - to his car's black leath - er seat.___ The

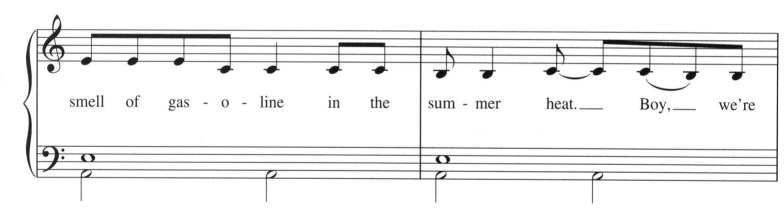

smell of gas - o - line in the sum - mer heat.___ Boy,___ we're

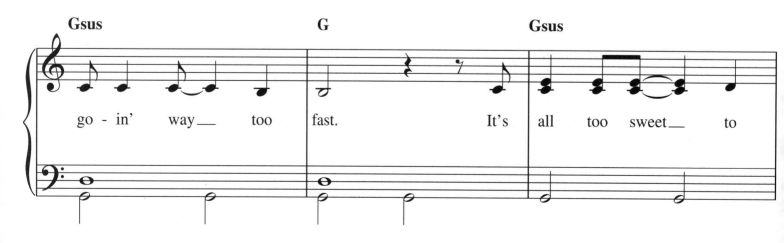

Gsus   **G**   **Gsus**

go - in' way___ too fast. It's all too sweet___ to

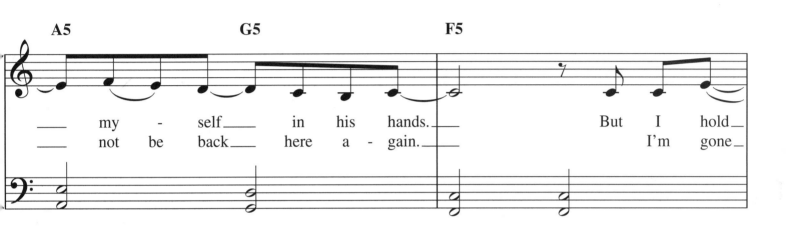

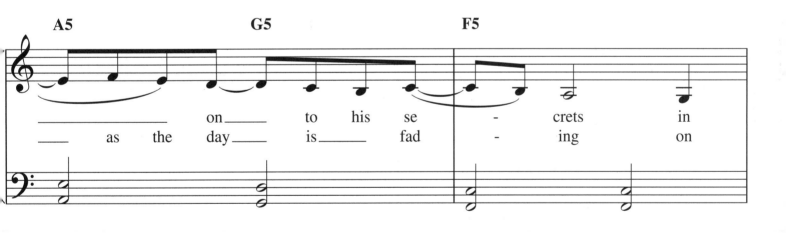

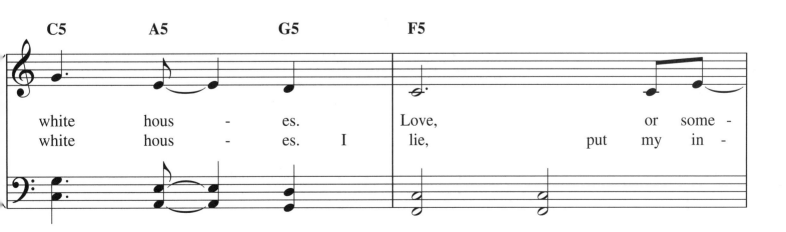

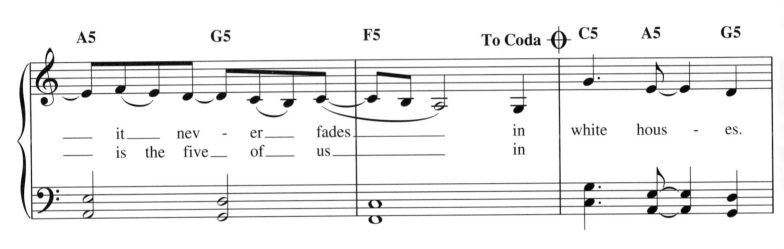

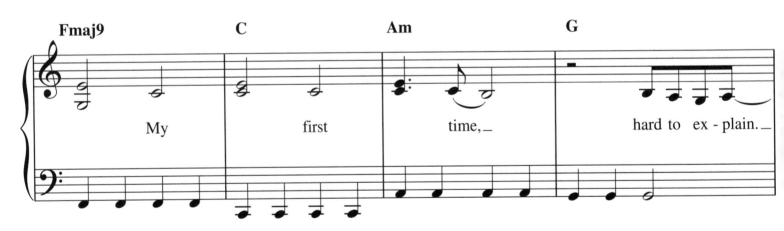

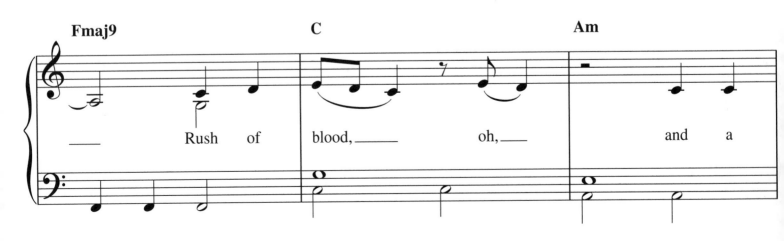

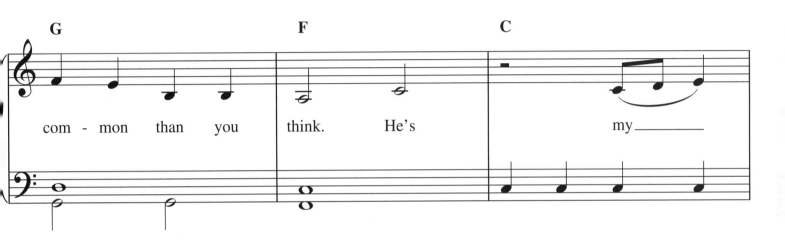

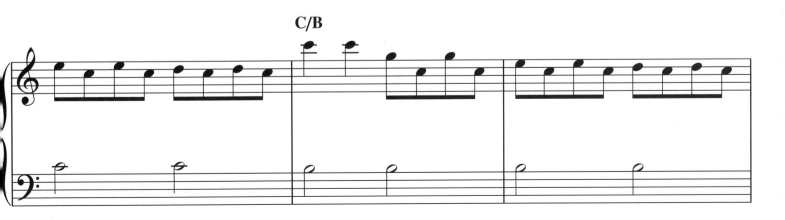

May-be you were all fast-er than me. We

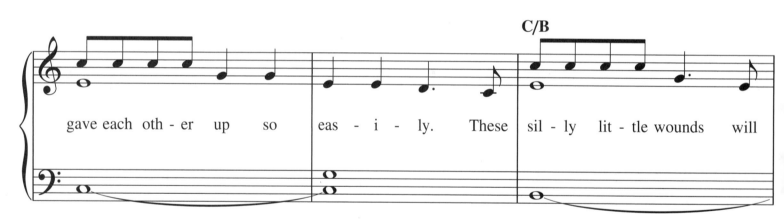

gave each oth-er up so eas-i-ly. These sil-ly lit-tle wounds will

D.S. al Coda

nev-er mend. I feel so far from where I've been._ So I go_

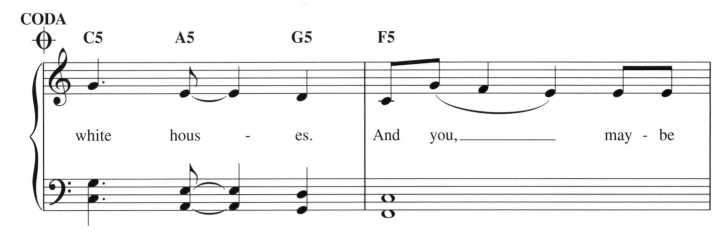

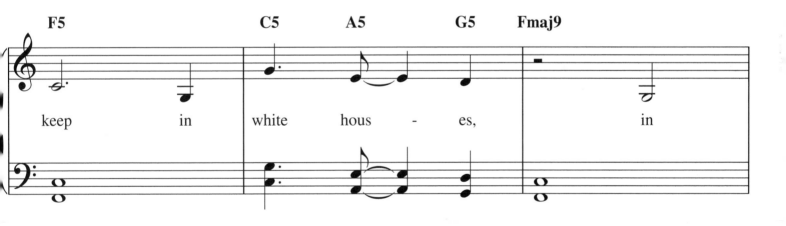

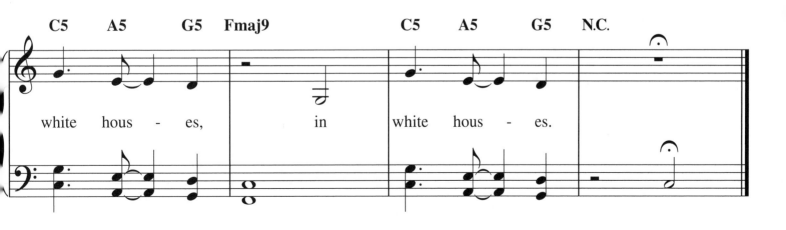

WE ARE NEVER EVER GETTING BACK TOGETHER

Words and Music by TAYLOR SWIFT,
SHELLBACK and MAX MARTIN

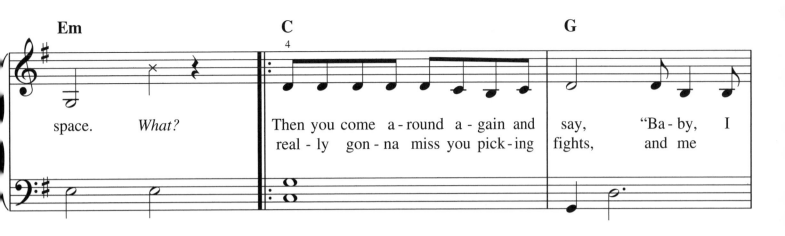

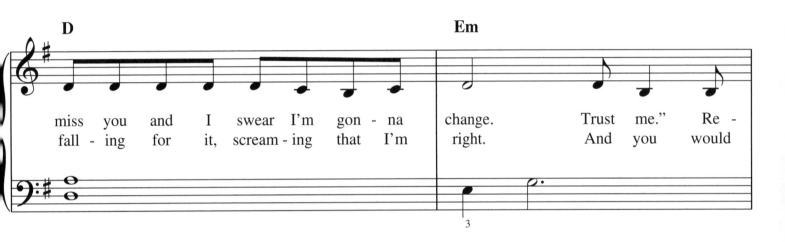

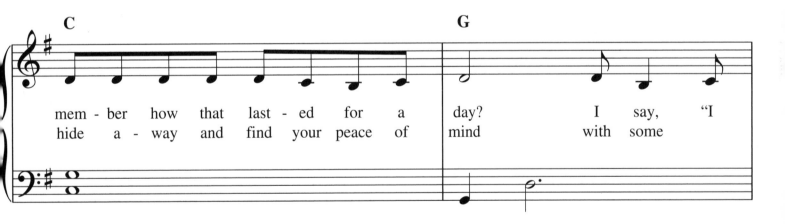

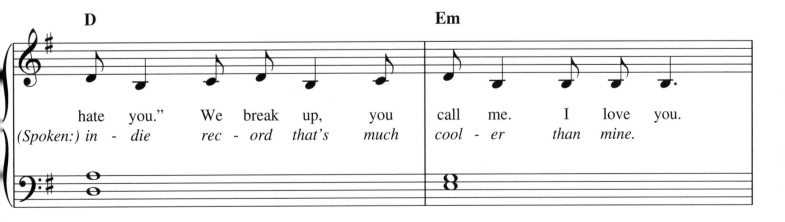

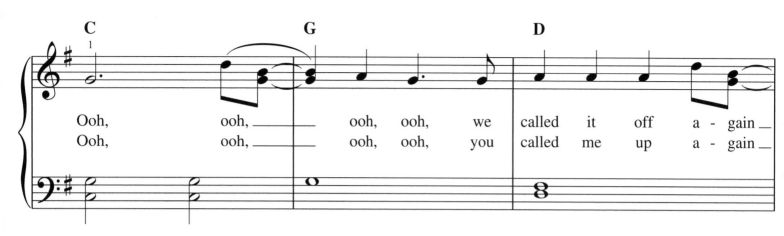

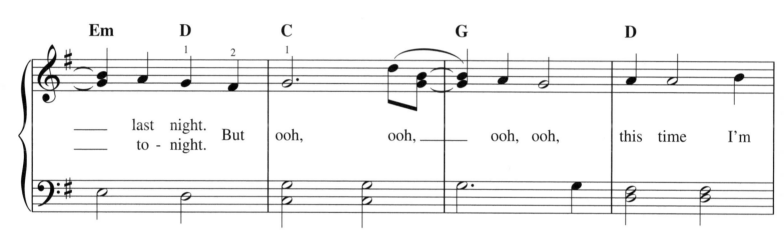

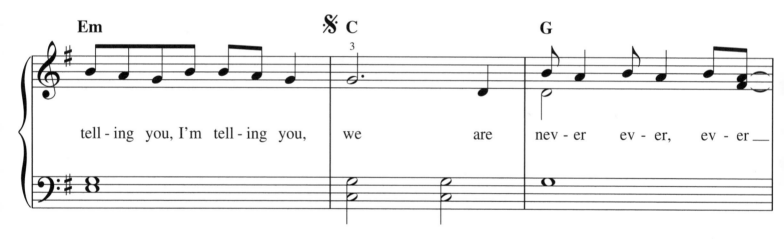

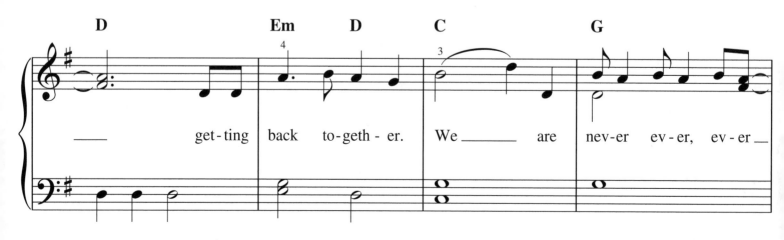

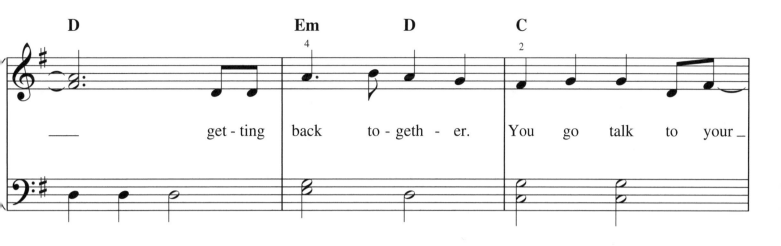

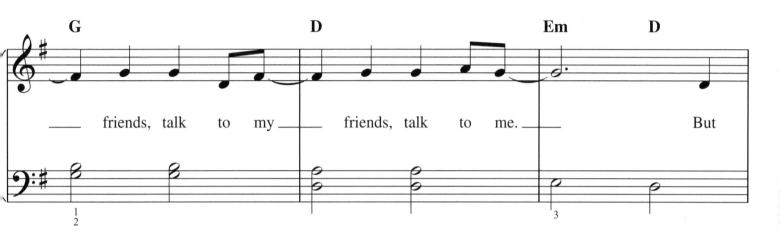

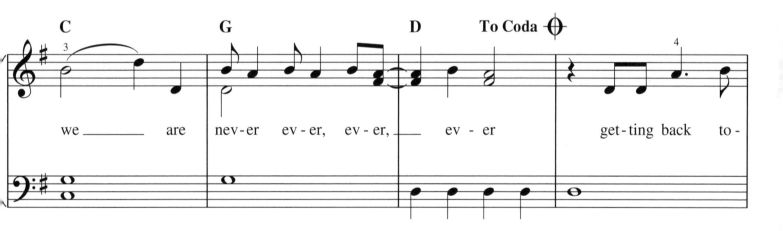

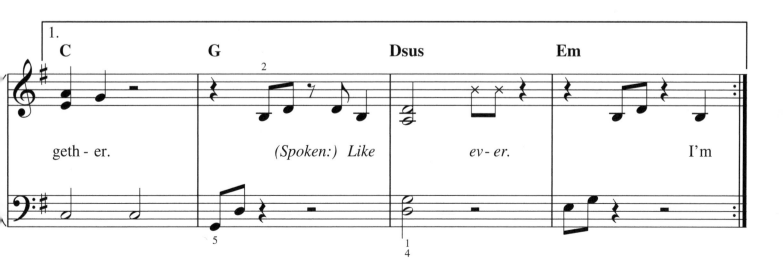

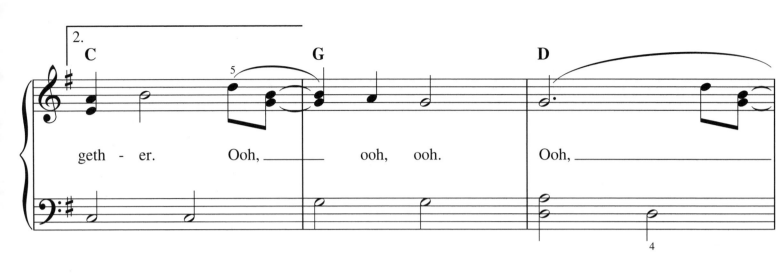

geth - er. Ooh, _____ ooh, ooh. Ooh, _____

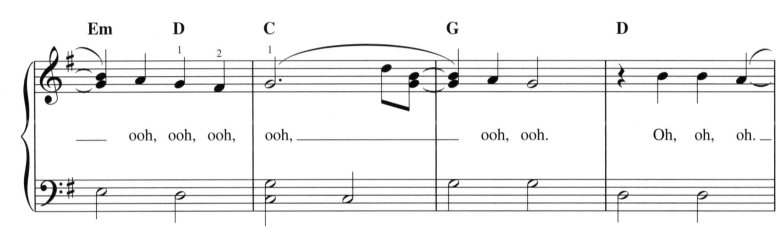

_____ ooh, ooh, ooh, ooh, _____ ooh, ooh. Oh, oh, oh. _____

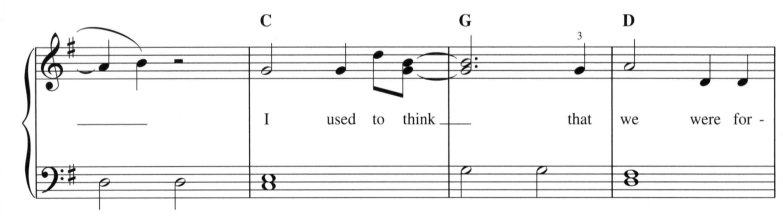

_____ I used to think _____ that we were for -

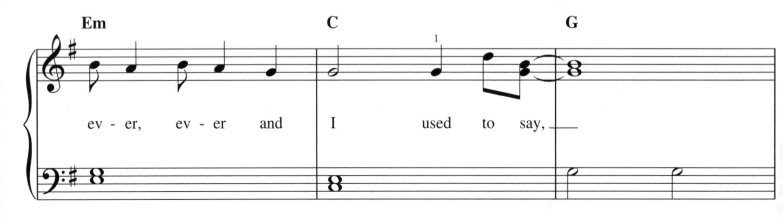

ev - er, ev - er and I used to say, _____

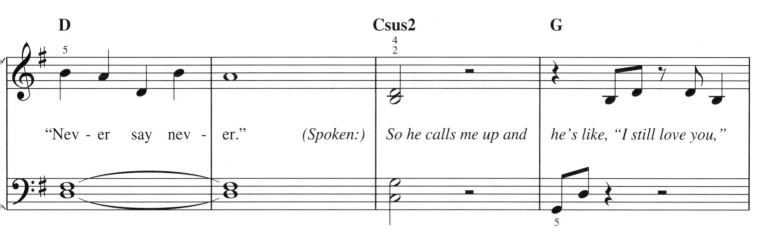

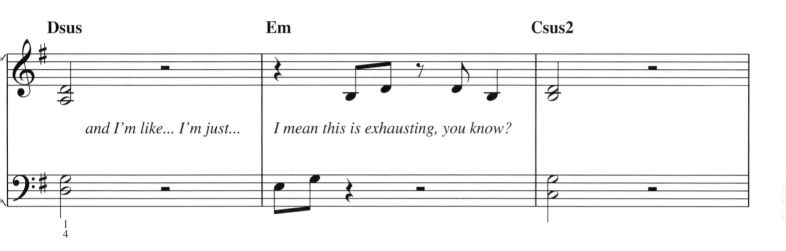

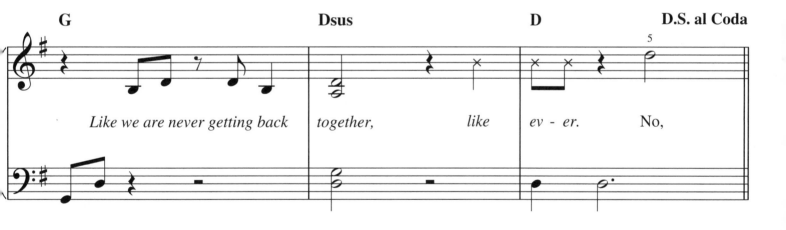

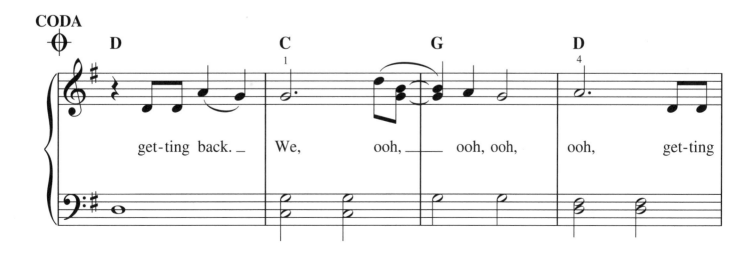